BLACKSTONE'S MODERN CARD TRICKS

by Harry Blackstone

NEW, REVISED EDITION

Melvin Powers
Wilshire Book Company

12015 Sherman Road, No. Hollywood, CA 91605

Published by arrangement with Doubleday & Company, Inc.

LIBRARY OF CONGRESS CATALOG CARD NUMBER 58–5566

COPYRIGHT © 1929, 1932 AND 1958 BY DOUBLEDAY & COMPANY, INC.

PRINTED IN THE UNITED STATES OF AMERICA

ISBN 0-87980-282-0

CONTENTS

Contents

INTRODUCTION

It is not difficult to perform tricks with cards. The old idea that considerable skill is necessary is now obsolete. Once, card tricks could be divided into two grand divisions—simple tricks and difficult tricks. The simple tricks were scarcely worthy of notice; the difficult ones were hard to learn. But that time has passed.

Many new and ingenious methods of card magic have been evolved. Older tricks have been improved beyond recognition. Some of the simpler sleights, formerly used but seldom, have now become adapted to newer purposes.

A certain amount of skill is required to do card tricks well. But it is a fact that such skill is scarcely more than is required to handle a pack of cards smoothly. Anyone who aspires to do card tricks at all will readily understand that the ability to shuffle a pack neatly and well is certainly a requirement.

Some of the cleverest tricks are really very simple. To make them effective, the magician must present them in a convincing fashion. If he appears clumsy, spectators will take it for granted that the tricks are simple. If he appears clever, spectators will believe that the tricks are the result of superior skill.

The essential thing, then, in learning card tricks, is to first familiarize oneself on the handling of a pack of cards. The beginner should spend some time in learning to shuffle rapidly—either by the dovetail method or by the overhand system, both of which are used by card players.

He should also try to deal cards smoothly and rapidly; learn to riffle the end of the pack; to spread the cards between his hands, or sweep them along the table. All these little points add to the effectiveness of a performance with cards.

It may be assumed that the average card player already knows how to handle a pack. If the reader possesses what we may term normal skill, he is ready to utilize the information which this book contains.

In the first section, we have introduced a number of sleights which will prove useful. Each one is included with a definite purpose—it has some use in connection with the tricks that appear in later sections. The reader should study it as preliminary work. He will find that most of the methods are merely ideas in card handling that will come easily to him. His study of that section need not be a long one. He can go on to the tricks that follow and refer back to the first section as needed.

The old idea of explaining card methods was to bewilder the student with some of the most difficult of all sleights, stating at the beginning that these must be learned in order to do card tricks. Such is not the plan in this book. The most difficult sleights are not included at all. The reader will find them in some of the older standard works on magic, if he chooses to look them up. They are useful to the expert card worker, but they are not needed by the average performer.

The right way to learn card tricks is to begin by doing them. This book follows that plan. At the same time, we advocate preliminary work with the cards themselves in order to present card tricks most effectively.

The first section—that of preliminary sleights—has been mentioned. The second section is a very useful one. Many good card tricks depend upon the location of a card which has been selected by a member of the audience. So our second section deals entirely with card locations. The performer can use whatever method he sees fit, choosing his favorite locations. Some are very easy of accomplishment and will enable the beginner to start using locations right away.

The third section covers card discoveries—unique ways of pro-

Introduction

ducing cards after one has been selected and located. It naturally follows the second section in logical sequence. The remaining sections involve tricks which do not require the usual locations and discoveries. Here the reader will find a varied array of card magic. The final section of the book covers tricks that utilize certain elements of skill, mostly referring back to the first section.

Special attention is called to the fourth section, which is devoted entirely to "spelling tricks"—a variety of card magic that has come into popularity during the past decade.

Harry Blackstone

BIOGRAPHICAL NOTE

For half a century the name Blackstone has symbolized Magic in the minds of the American public. Today thousands of magical enthusiasts date their interest in the mystic art from the time they first saw Blackstone on the stage. This is indeed appropriate, for Harry Blackstone himself gained his inspiration when he witnessed a performance by the Great Kellar at McVicker's Theatre in Chicago.

After rising to be a headliner in the days of vaudeville, Blackstone expanded his show to full evening proportions, and during World War II he toured the military bases with a complete magical extravaganza, requiring a company of more than thirty persons. In subsequent years he played all the leading theaters of the United States and Canada, from coast to coast, with his "Show of 1001 Wonders."

The thousand and first wonder was Blackstone himself, the white-haired wizard who can perform every type of magic from deft, close-up sleights with cards, to sawing a girl in half with an electric buzz saw, yet restoring her without a scratch. It was such versatility that won Blackstone the rating of "America's Number One Magician"—a title which he still retains.

Esteemed by fellow members of his craft, Blackstone was elected president of the Magicians' Guild of America, and has contributed greatly to the success of that organization. Today still another generation is witnessing Blackstone's Magic through the medium of television, as the Maestro of Mystery is featured on many TV programs.

Walter B. Gibson

Chapter I

PRELIMINARY SLEIGHTS

Here the reader will find useful methods in card handling that he can apply constantly in card tricks. The first of these are false shuffles and false cuts—always of value.

The other sleights in this section have been included because they are of use in certain tricks which could not otherwise be performed successfully. With the present trend of card magic, there is no purpose in utilizing all sorts of manipulations. Nevertheless, certain tricks require the introduction of some bit of skill.

The reader should familiarize himself with all of the methods given in this section so he can refer to them as he proceeds. If he likes a particular trick that depends upon the "glide" or the "palm," he can then spend time in practicing the sleight.

Any feats of skill with cards are useful, as they represent a definite step in the smooth handling of cards. At the same time, the old idea of practicing sleights that had no practical use is something which can scarcely be recommended. The sleights in this section were placed there after the major portion of the book had been written and they were found to be necessary for reference in certain tricks.

1. FALSE SHUFFLES

False shuffles are useful in connection with many card tricks. Through their aid, the performer can keep a card on the top or bottom of the pack; or can retain the entire deck in its regular order.

Such shuffles are not difficult to learn, although they should be practiced frequently. They must simulate genuine shuffles; therefore, some of the best false shuffles are patterned directly after ordinary ways of shuffling the pack.

In Chapter VIII of this book, you will find a false shuffling system for use with the "Card Control." Other methods of false shuffling are given here, with a few references to the system described in full detail in a later chapter. There is no reason why any performer should attempt to utilize a wide variety of false shuffles. The shuffle is simply used to mix the cards—and it is natural for a person to shuffle the cards in one way. The magician, therefore, is apt to bring suspicion upon himself if he shuffles differently each time he handles the cards.

Most persons, however, utilize both the dovetail shuffle and the overhand shuffle, as well as cuts, when they are mixing the cards. Therefore we are giving practical methods of false shuffling both dovetail and overhand, with a section on false cuts in addition.

2. DOVETAIL FALSE SHUFFLES

In the dovetail shuffle, the executor simply divides the pack into two portions and riffles the ends, allowing the two sections of the pack to interweave. In doing this, it is best to let the inner corners of the packets run together, under control of the thumbs.

In many tricks, the magician desires to keep the top card in its position; in others, he may wish to keep the bottom card in position. This is easy with the dovetail shuffle—in fact it is so natural that there is virtually no falsity about the shuffle.

To keep the top card in position, simply dovetail in the usual fashion, but be sure to retain the top card until after all others have fallen. By this method, one can keep a dozen cards or more on top of the pack. Presuming that the upper portion of the pack is taken in the right hand, it is desirable that the upper portion should be slightly larger than the lower. By riffling the lower portion more rapidly than the upper, the left hand finishes with its cards while those in the right are still being riffled. The top cards remain on top.

To retain the bottom cards in position, they are simply allowed to fall first. In this case, the left hand, with the bottom heap, runs ahead of the right, dropping a number of cards before the right hand begins its release.

Retaining cards on both top and bottom is simplicity with the dovetail shuffle. Dividing the pack into two equal heaps, the left hand lets the lower cards go first; then the right hand follows and when the left hand packet is exhausted, the right hand is still riffling cards.

The ordinary false shuffle by the dovetail method is scarcely more than an imperfect shuffle which the performer turns to his own advantage. Yet the spectators, unsuspecting of his purpose, have no idea that he is deliberately controlling the cards.

3. COMPLETE PACK CONTROL
(*With the Dovetail*)

The apparent shuffling of the pack without disturbing the arrangement of a single card may be accomplished with the dovetail shuffle. This is a real false shuffle. It will require considerable practice, in order to render it deceptive.

The right hand heap represents the upper portion of the pack. It should contain fewer cards than the left hand heap. Cards are riffled first from the left hand, giving that packet a start. Following, the right hand ends with some of its cards on top of the pack.

Up to this point the shuffle is genuine. The spectators are allowed to see that the inner corners of the pack are actually dovetailed. Only the very corners are interlaced, however. As though to complete the shuffle, the performer swings his fingers together. As he does so, he bends the outer end of the right portion upward. The fingers come together and by a slight drawing of the thumbs, the interwoven corners of the pack are separated.

The upward bend of the outer corner of the right heap enables it to slide up on top of the left heap and thus the hands come together, simulating exactly the completion of an ordinary dovetail shuffle. The fingers prevent anyone from observing that the shuffle is not bona fide.

This shuffle should be practiced until it is natural. It reaches a point where just the slightest twist enables the magician to change a genuine shuffle into a false one. By using this mode of shuffling regularly, he can make the movement highly convincing, no matter how closely the observers may happen to be watching.

4. OVERHAND FALSE SHUFFLE

(*To Control Bottom Cards*)

In the simplest and most natural form of the overhand shuffle, the shuffler holds the deck in his left hand and peels off several cards with the thumb. The remainder of the pack is brought down by the right hand and more cards are peeled off. This is continued until all the cards have been shuffled off.

To control bottom cards during a normal overhand shuffle, the performer simply grips them with the tips of his left fingers when the left thumb peels off the first layer of cards. Result: the bottom cards are retained beneath the top ones. The rest of the pack is shuffled on top and the bottom cards are not disturbed.

By this method the performer can control a single bottom card and also bring a card from the top to go with it. He does this by peeling away the lone top card and shuffling the rest of the pack on it. He retains the bottom card when he draws down the top one. This shuffle is executed with the left side toward the audience.

5. OVERHAND FALSE SHUFFLE

(*To Control Top Cards*)

In this false shuffle, the performer stands with his right side toward the audience and holds the pack in his left hand. The top of the pack is against the fingers of the left hand.

In shuffling, the pack is lifted by the right hand. The left thumb peels off a few of the bottom cards, while the left fingers retain some of the top ones. The pack is brought toward the left thumb,

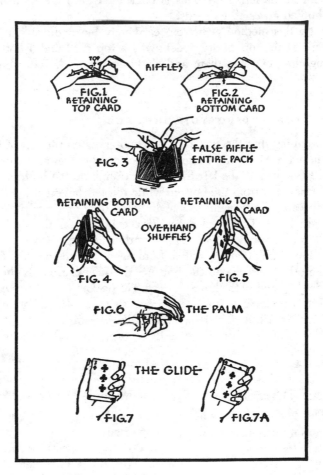

The diagrams show the correct positions for various preliminary sleights explained in Section One.

which peels away cards and adds them to the bottom of the cluster held in the left hand. This is continued until the right hand has shuffled away all its cards.

By this method, a bottom card may be made to join a single card at the top. Simply peel away a top card and a bottom card together, clipping them and shuffling the pack upon the bottom card.

6. TOP AND BOTTOM SHUFFLE

Assuming that the magician has two cards on the top of the pack and wishes to transfer one to the bottom, he does as follows: Holding the pack in the left hand, with thumb on the bottom, he peels a few cards from the bottom while the left fingers draw down one top card. He then shuffles away until only one card is left in the right hand. That card drops on the bottom of the pack. One of the top cards is still on top; the other on the bottom.

Presuming that one of two bottom cards is to go to the top while the other remains on the bottom, the magician holds the pack in his left hand with thumb on top. He peels off some top cards and draws a single bottom card beneath them. He then shuffles the pack from the right hand until only one card is left. It goes on top. Thus one bottom card is on top; the other remains on the bottom.

7. ·OVERHAND SHUFFLE WITH COMPLETE PACK

This is the method whereby none of the cards are disturbed during an overhand shuffle. Hold the pack in the left hand with the thumb on top. Peel off about a dozen cards with the left thumb. Bring the pack down on top of those cards and remove no cards whatever—although the motion makes it appear that you do.

Now bring the pack beneath the left hand cards and peel off some with the left thumb. Once more come on top with the right hand but leave none. Go beneath and leave some. Continue thus as though you were leaving cards on both top and bottom. Actually you are leaving them on the bottom only. In this way the entire pack is shuffled off—right back to its original condition, without a single card being disturbed.

This shuffle naturally keeps top and bottom cards in position, so it can be used for that purpose as well as for an entire deck shuffle.

8. FALSE CUTS

A false cut serves the same purpose as the false shuffle—an apparent mixing of the pack without the mixing taking place. The usual false cut is designed to preserve the entire arrangement of the pack.

It is a simple fact that a single cut does not disturb the order of the cards, even though it does change the position of the top card. Therefore false cuts are designed to appear more thorough than a single cut but to do no more than cut the card once.

Many of the tricks in this book involve selected cards that are on the top of the pack or the bottom; therefore the false cuts have been specially arranged so that they do not make any change at all. Despite their appearance, they leave the pack exactly as it was before the cuts were made.

Therefore these cuts, when learned, can be applied in any trick. The card conjuror may at any time give the pack a series of cuts and be sure that he is not injuring his chances of doing the trick successfully.

Many magicians neglect false cuts. This is a mistake. In all legerdemain with cards—particularly when tricks are performed at close range—false cuts add that degree of emphasis that makes the magician's work seem amazing. Furthermore, false cuts can be learned easily and done with great rapidity—even by the beginner.

9. SIMPLE FALSE CUT
(*With Three Heaps*)

Lay the pack on the table. Lift off about two-thirds of the cards and lay this portion six inches to the right. Lift off half of this portion and place it in the center. This makes three piles.

Put the right pile on the left. Put the center pile on top. This brings the pack back to its original position. The following table shows the piles as they are made:

1	3	2
(Bottom)	(Top)	(Middle)

2 goes on 1 and 3 goes on 2. The pack is unchanged. This is ordinarily done with one hand. With two hands, form the piles with the right hand only. Then reach across with the left and pick up heap 2, dropping it on heap 1. The right hand immediately picks up 3 and puts it on 1 and 2.

10. ANOTHER FALSE CUT

(*With Four Heaps*)

Lay the pack on the table and lift off most of the cards, leaving a small heap. Drop a dozen more from the bottom, to the right of the first pile. Drop a dozen more below the first pile and put the remainder at the right. Thus:

1	2
(Bottom)	(Lower Middle)
3	4
(Upper Middle)	(Top)

Gathering: Place 3 on 2; put 4 on 2 and 3. Lay all on 1. With two hands, the left hand picks up 3, dropping it on 2; the right hand picks up 4, gathers 2 and 3 beneath it and transfers all to the top of 1.

11. SPECIAL FALSE CUT

(*With Five Heaps*)

This time four heaps are formed about the pack as a center, making five heaps in all. The mode of cutting is different at the start. A few cards are lifted from the pack and laid at the upper left corner of an imaginary square. Some more are taken from the pack and put at the upper right corner. Another group from the pack is placed at the lower left; a fourth group at the lower right.

This is the arrangement:

1	2
(Top)	(Second)
*	
(Pack)	
3	4
(Third)	(Fourth)

Gathering: Drop 2 on 3. Drop 1 on 2 and 3. Drop 4 on pack. Place 1, 2, 3 on 4 and pack.

With two hands, the left drops 1, the right 2, the left 3, the right 4. Picking up; right places 2 on 3; left puts 1 on 2; right places 4 on pack; left puts 1, 2, 3 on 4 and pack.

12. SHUFFLE CUT

This cut has the appearance of a shuffle and certainly gives the impression of a mixing of the cards. It may be performed either

SHUFFLE CUT

The positions of the pack during the stages of the Shuffle Cut:
1 shows the original top section; 2 the center; 3 the bottom.

with the cards on the table or with the cards held by the hands alone.

The hands hold the ends of the pack. Fingers are at the far side; thumbs at the near side. The right hand draws off cards from the bottom, pulling them away between the thumb and forefinger alone. Moving above the pack, carrying its heap, the right hand grasps some of the top cards between the tip of the thumb and the second finger.

These are drawn off to the right also—the position enables the right hand to keep the two groups separated. The left hand now holds a group of cards—those which constitute the center portion of the pack.

The left hand comes above and places its cards upon the upper group held by the right hand. The left draws away both groups as one. The right hand then lays its only remaining group upon the cards that are in the left hand.

With a little practice, this procedure becomes simple. Learn to do it rapidly and it is very effective. It can be repeated time and again, for it brings the pack back to the starting point. No change whatever in the order of the cards.

13. FALSE CUT SHIFT

In this method of locating a chosen card, a false cut serves the purpose of a pass. The cut is very similar to the "Shuffle Cut" elsewhere described. It is given here in detail and the reader will note the similarity.

The pack is held between the tips of thumbs and fingers. The right hand is near one end of the pack; the left near the other.

The right hand draws off the lower half of the pack between the thumb and forefinger, inviting the return of the selected card, which is placed on the lower half of the pack.

The right hand then moves above the pack and draws off the upper portion between its thumb and second finger—below the portion already held. These sections of the pack are kept separate.

Left hand is now holding the center portion of the pack between thumb and forefinger. It comes above and with thumb and second finger draws off the upper of the two groups held by the right hand. It keeps its groups separated.

The right hand drops its one remaining group of cards upon the upper group held by the left hand and pulls away both groups as one. This leaves the left hand with its lower, single group, which it drops upon the cards in the right hand.

This puts the selected card on top of the pack, in spite of the confusing shuffle cut.

14. THE REVOLVING PASS

The sleight known as the "pass" is nothing more than an invisible cut used by the magician to transpose two portions of the pack. It was for many years the recognized method of bringing a chosen card to the top of the pack.

REVOLVING PASS

The upper half of the pack is dropped face up on the right fingers. Note how the left fingers flip it over. The lower diagrams show the other half of the pack following.

The difficulty of learning the "pass" is out of proportion to the value of the sleight, so far as the average card performer is concerned. With all the modern card detections and locations that have been devised, the "pass" is necessary only on rare occasions.

There are various forms of the "pass"—and the really good ones are hard to learn. But there are also certain "false passes" which accomplish the same purpose. The one we are about to describe is easy to do and is, at the same time, deceptive. It would not be a good sleight to use repeatedly; but it is excellent when performed occasionally.

It is included in this book so that the reader may have it available when the "pass" is actually required in any particular trick, unless he happens to be familiar with some other form of the "pass" which he finds suited to his purpose.

Hold the pack in the left hand, thumb on top, fingers beneath. The little finger is inserted in the pack at the lower right corner, holding the two portions of the pack separated. Thus, if a chosen card has been replaced in the pack, that card is just beneath the tip of the left little finger.

The right hand approaches the left. The left hand tilts toward it and lets the upper portion of the pack fall face up upon the tips of the right fingers. The left side of the portion is resting on the tips of the left fingers also (with the exception of the left little finger, which, with the left thumb, holds the lower half of the pack).

Now the left fingers give the upper portion an added flip, causing it to fall face downward in the palm of the right hand.

The right thumb now gives the bottom portion a flip from beneath so that it drops upon the finger tips of both hands, face up —just as the first heap did. Again the left fingers flip, turning this heap over. It lands upon the upper portion, in the right hand.

The procedure requires four movements. Each half of the pack, in turn, does a complete revolution. The upshot is that the lower heap is on top of the upper heap. The "pass" has been accomplished.

The effect is highly deceptive. There is no attempt to conceal the motion. On the contrary, it should be done boldly, in full view. It appears to be a fancy action like a riffle—a bit of jugglery that adds to the trick and seems a display of skill. It has a peculiar effect, no one realizing that it actually cuts the pack.

In using this revolving pass, the performer should first square up the pack at the front, so no one will notice the little finger of the left hand, inserted at the inner end of the pack. Then the right hand riffles the outer end of the pack, to indicate that all is fair. Immediately after the riffle comes the revolving pass.

There is no great skill needed; but the move should be practiced until the four motions blend into one, making a very pretty continuous effect. It is quite possible to throw the cards from hand to hand, letting each portion revolve as it goes from left to right. This is also a pretty effect.

The important point to remember is that the movement is actually used to transpose the sections of the pack; and it serves that purpose admirably. By using fancy cuts and riffles in other tricks, the magician can lead his observers to expect little flourishes that have no particular bearing on the trick; and when he uses the revolving pass, they will be taken entirely unaware.

15. THE PALM

One of the most useful of all card sleights is the "palm" by which a card is removed from the pack and secretly retained in the right hand. Sometimes two or more cards may be retained in this manner.

The simplest palm for a single card is the following. Hold the pack in the left hand, flat and back upward. Place the right forefinger against the outer left corner of the pack. The joint of the finger should touch the corner of the card.

The right fingers are all together. Lined in this fashion, they move forward, taking the card with them. The hand closes slightly and the fingers point downward as they go along, so that the end of the pack presses against the end of the card and it is forced tightly into the right hand.

The hand should be kept in a half-closed position, retaining the palmed card. This method enables the hand to get a firm hold on the card. The pressure should be light at first, however, so that only one card will follow the right hand.

To palm one card or more—a required number—the left thumb first pushes the cards to the right side of the pack. As the right hand covers the pack, as though to square the cards, the second finger of the left hand pushes upward from beneath and forces the cards into the right palm. This must be done neatly, to make sure that the cards are well hidden in the right hand.

16. THE GLIDE

The "glide" is a very old sleight—but a very useful one and a very easy one. It was first described many years ago and it served its purposes then; however, newer tricks have utilized this sleight and it is because of this that we recommend the method to the reader.

The "glide" is actually a "second deal" in which the cards are drawn from the bottom of the pack instead of the top. It is of use only to magicians and it takes the place of a card "change."

There are two methods for the "glide." The first is the neater; the second the easier.

First Method: Hold the pack in the left hand, the thumb at the right side, the fingers curled beneath, at the left. The bulk of the hand is above the pack, which is face down. Show the bottom card by tilting up the pack. Hold the pack face down, while the right hand approaches the outer end to draw off the bottom card.

At this point, the left third finger gets busy. It moves inward and slides the bottom card along with it. Hence the right hand, in drawing off a card, is able to take the second card from the bottom—not the bottom card itself. The right hand deals the card face downward on the table and everyone supposes it to be the card that was shown on the bottom of the pack.

Moistening the left third finger will facilitate the operation of the "glide."

With this sleight, the magician can "change" a card or he can make a chosen card appear at any number from the bottom of the pack, simply by holding it back while others are drawn forth.

Second Method: This time, the right fingers do the work. The right hand approaches the outer end of the pack. The thumb rests on top; the fingers beneath. The right fingers push the bottom card back; then draw off the next card.

In both methods, the card can be drawn, when required, by the right fingers. If they want the pulled-back card, they simply stretch to get it and bring it out.

The "glide," while an easy sleight in either form, should not be neglected in practice. Its effectiveness depends upon doing it neatly. Fumbling will spoil any trick, and simply because the sleight is not hard to learn is no reason for performing it crudely.

17. THE FALSE COUNT

A very simple and useful sleight. The performer wishes to count off some cards from the top of the pack and to actually take less than the audience supposes.

He does it thus. He draws off one card, saying "one." He places the card back on the pack and removes another with it, counting "two." The left thumb pushes each card to the right to assist the right hand in the removal.

In taking a third card, the magician simulates the previous movement, but he simply brushes the right hand cards upon the card that is on the pack, without removing it. The left thumb, at the same time, pulls back the card.

By this procedure, the magician can apparently count off twelve cards, really taking only nine. Three times during the course of the counting, the false motion is made.

With nine cards in his hand, the magician can count the packet to make it appear as twelve. He simply counts off three cards normally; makes the false count on number four; actually counts off the next card; then the false count; counts off another; then the false count; and finally counts off the remainder.

Make sure of the position of the cards, remembering that they are backs up. Practice the sleight, until you can do it naturally and easily. You will be surprised how simple it is—and how deceptive.

Chapter II

CARD LOCATIONS

In locating cards, there are certain points to be considered. A card, having been selected and replaced in the pack, is presumably lost. The chances of finding it again are—from the spectator's view—just about one in fifty-two.

It is true that very many tricks begin with the old formula: "Take a card." Perhaps the phrase has become hackneyed. Nevertheless, it is the usual beginning of many good tricks. If people want to see card tricks, they should expect to take cards.

After the card is taken, it is up to the performer to find it when needed. Card locations solve that problem. There are various types of locations. We can consider them in three groups.

First: The learning of a card. Through some method, the performer discovers the card by glancing through the pack after the card has been returned. This type of location is sometimes termed a "detection." It is not so effective as the controlling of a card, but it serves as well in certain tricks.

Second: The control of a card. The performer, by some system, keeps the card under his control, bringing it either to the top or the bottom of the pack. He does not necessarily know the name of the card. This type of location is usually followed by false shuffling.

Third: The forcing of a card. In this type of location the magician knows beforehand what card the spectator is going to take. The "force" serves purposes all its own. By use of it, the magician can predict the name of a card which is to be selected. The "force" also serves as a location, however, for it enables the magician to find a card any time after it is returned to the pack.

The special advantage of the "force" in locating cards is that with it, the spectators may be allowed to shuffle the pack themselves, thus strengthening the performer's own position when he shuffles for himself. This is also possible with a form of location known as the "glimpse," which is explained in this section.

Often, when the performer knows the name of a card, he can find it by the simple expedient of shuffling the pack dovetail fashion. He riffles the end of the pack that is toward himself and thus sights the card as it comes along. Cutting at that point, he can keep the card on the bottom or the top as he prefers.

This is a useful point to know in connection with card tricks where the performer is using some form of location other than the actual control of a chosen card.

1. THE DIVIDED PACK

This is one of the simplest forms of card location ever devised. In fact, it is so simple that it has been relegated to beginners and its real merits have been forgotten.

Red and Black

To explain the method in its primitive form requires only a few words. The pack is cut into two heaps. A card is selected at random from one heap. It is placed in the other heap. Looking through the second heap, the magician discovers the chosen card.

This is easy to do when one knows how the pack is divided. One heap contains red cards; the other heap contains black. Simple, isn't it? A red card shows up among the blacks or a black shows up among the reds—as the case may be.

Note that each heap may be shuffled prior to the drawing of a card. But should any spectator chance to look at the cards in his heap, he would easily find a clue to the trick.

Mixed Suits

When we consider this idea in its more subtle forms, we discover real merit in it. The first stunt is to use the spades and hearts (mixed) in one heap; the clubs and diamonds (mixed) in the other. This means that a much closer inspection is necessary on the part of the spectator.

Odd and Even

A further improvement is to pay no attention to suit whatever. Use all *odd* cards (ace, three, five, seven, nine, jack, king) in one heap; use all *even* cards (two, four, six, eight, ten, queen) in the other. That makes detection highly unlikely.

Mixed Odds and Evens

In its most elaborated form, the trick utilizes the *even* spades and hearts and the *odd* clubs and diamonds in one heap; the other heap consists of the *odd* spades and hearts and the *even* clubs and diamonds. This makes the system virtually undetectable.

For practical purposes, however, the use of odds in one section and evens in the other will be all that the performer may require.

Now it is obvious that the trick will work both ways: given two heaps of different kinds of cards, one or more cards may be transferred from heap A to heap B; or from heap B to heap A. Examination of both heaps will show any "strangers" in their midst. Thus the performer is not limited to the choice of a single card.

Complete Pack Method

Let us consider the two-heap idea with the pack all together. The top portion of the pack consists of, say, odds. The lower portion consists of evens. Spreading the pack, the magician requests the selection of a card. If one is taken from the top half of the pack, he keeps on spreading and allows the card to be put back in the bottom part. If one is taken from the bottom portion, the pack is closed and spread again near the top, so the card goes in there. This is done with two or more cards; then the pack is cut a few times. Upon looking at the faces of the cards—even while the spectators are watching—the magician can immediately find the chosen cards.

Complete Pack with Shuffles

To make the trick more deceptive, we shall explain a way of using this principle in which the pack is genuinely cut in four heaps before the selection of cards; and actually shuffled in dovetail fashion after the chosen cards are replaced!

Arrange group A (consisting of even reds and odd blacks) on top of group B (consisting of odd reds and even blacks). Remember the bottom card of group A—say the ten of diamonds. Or the joker may be placed at that point.

Spread the pack slightly and cut at the key card. That makes two heaps, A and B. Cut each of those heaps, making two A heaps and two B heaps. In assembling, gather the heaps A, B, A, B from bottom to top. The A heap with the ten of diamonds should be the upper A heap. Also note the bottom card of the upper B heap.

Now cards are selected and replaced. This time, you are dealing with four groups. They must be considered as the cards are replaced. Simply see to it that the card goes in a group of the other variety.

When the chosen cards are back in the pack, spread a trifle to find the ten of diamonds and cut there. Now, in dovetailing, let the right hand cards drop more rapidly than the left. As soon as the bottom card of the upper B heap (say the four of spades) appears, retain it and let the left hand cards fall until they are well exhausted. Then finish the shuffle. This simply segregates the A and B heaps. You are ready to look for the chosen cards.

2. THE NEW PACK

This is one of those opportune tricks that no card conjuror should neglect when the occasion permits it. It is particularly useful when performing at a card table. A new pack is often presented to the magician and then he has his chance.

A pack of cards is taken from the case. It is spread along the table. Persons are asked to draw cards. The magician's head is turned away. As soon as cards have been removed, he closes the pack without looking at it—sweeping the cards together.

Again he spreads the pack and asks for the replacement of the chosen cards. This being done, he sweeps the pack up without even glancing at it.

Nothing could seem fairer than this. The magician does not even know how many cards were chosen. But by spreading the pack before him and concentrating, he manages to remove several cards, which he lays faces down. The chosen cards are named. Those cards are turned up. They are the chosen ones!

New packs are always arranged in sequence of suits. Nowadays the suits are usually in order from ace to king. Thus when cards are taken—the pack closed—the pack reopened—the selected cards naturally go back at new positions and it is a simple matter to learn their identity by simply looking through the pack! For they are out of place.

The pack may be cut once or twice during the trick; that does not disturb the rotation. Afterward, the pack should be shuffled immediately to dispose of the clue that would give away the method.

3. EASY LOCATIONS

(With Puzzling Additions)

Bottom Card Location

This is one of the oldest types of card location. We are describing it, however, because it has many useful variations and can be made to deceive the shrewdest spectator if handled in the proper manner.

Basically, the trick is simply a division of the pack into two heaps. A card is taken from the top of the lower heap, noted, and transferred to the upper heap. The cut is then completed. After a few cuts of the pack, the magician looks through the cards and discovers the selected one.

This is accomplished by first sighting the bottom card of the pack. When the selected card is transferred from the lower heap to the upper and the cut completed, the known (bottom) card naturally comes on top of the selected card. Cutting does not separate those two cards. It is easy for the magician to discover the chosen card.

Top Card Location

Now let us note some variations to this idea which the average man of a few card tricks does not know. First is the subterfuge of noting the *top* card of the pack instead of the bottom. To facilitate this, the magician may actually note the bottom card and shuffle it to the top before placing the pack on the table. The pack is cut; it is divided into two heaps. A card is noted while being transferred from the lower heap to the upper. The magician tells the spectator to complete the cut—and requests him to mix the cards of the lower heap before he does so!

The shuffle puts the bottom card out of commission and kills the spectator's pet theory (if he has it) that the bottom card is of help to the magician.

Top and Bottom Location

Another factor which is not realized—even by magicians—is that the pack can be shuffled when the bottom card or the top card serve as locators. Yes, it can be shuffled—if you pick your shuffler.

The average person does not shuffle a pack thoroughly. Noting such a person, the magician can give him the pack for shuffling and the chances of the two cards (locator and chosen) being separated is very slight. This applies to those who shuffle by the overhand method. The dovetail shuffle, if thorough, is more apt to spoil the trick.

But this leads us to the combined location in which the magician knows *both* the top card and the bottom one. When the pack is cut into two heaps and the chosen card transferred from lower to upper, the completion of the cut puts it *between* two known cards.

The magician can either find it as the card above the original top card or the card below the original bottom card. In other words, the wizard has caused the formation of a little cluster of three cards—the center one being the selected card.

Ordinary shuffling is not apt to disturb this group. Upon looking through the pack, the magician will usually find the desired card right between the other two. But supposing the shuffle is quite a thorough one. The chosen card may drift away from one of its locators, but it has very little chance of leaving both of them.

For instance: let us consider a group formed by the six of spades, ace of hearts and six of diamonds (from top to bottom). The six of spades is the original bottom card; the ace of hearts is the chosen card; the six of diamonds is the original top card. If the cards appear in that position after the shuffle, it is obvious that the ace of hearts is the card the magician wants.

Now suppose he finds the two locating sixes well apart. Beneath the six of spades is the king of clubs; above the six of diamonds is the ace of hearts. He knows that the chosen card is either the king of clubs or the ace of hearts. The magician then uses both those cards in whatever trick he is performing. For instance, he can slide one card to the top of the pack and the other to the bottom. Then he strikes the pack and turns up the top card. If it is recognized as the chosen card, well and good. If not, the magician "remembers" that the blow knocks the card to the bottom —not to the top, so he shows the bottom card to be the chosen one.

4. THE MASTER CARD LOCATION

This trick was highly advertised when it appeared a few years ago and it is still known to only a very few. It is a most convincing method of discovering a chosen card. The pack is shuffled by a spectator. The magician spreads the pack face down. A spectator touches a card. Before he has a chance to remove it, the magician puts the pack right in the spectator's hands and lets him turn up the card while the pack is in his own possession. He does not even remove the card from the pack. Then he cuts the pack as often as he wishes; yet the magician, looking through the pack, learns the name of the selected card.

The operation is quite ingenious. Upon receiving the shuffled pack, the magician notes the bottom card by turning the pack slightly toward himself. He begins to spread the cards from hand to hand. He counts them as he does so. Thus, when the spectator touches a card, the magician knows just how far down it is from the top.

He gives out the pack with impunity. For so long as the spectator cuts the cards with single cuts only, the selected card will always be the same number below the card that was on the bottom of the pack—the number counted from the bottom!

All the magician has to do when he gets the pack is spread the cards with the faces toward himself. He looks for the card he knows (the original bottom card) and counts down to the selected card. If he comes to the bottom of the pack during his count, he continues the count from the top.

Cutting the pack—in single cuts—does not change the rotation and the relationship of the known card to the chosen one will remain a constant number.

In utilizing this card location, the performer should practice counting cards as he spreads them. There is much to be gained by doing the counting in a rapid, smooth manner. With a little practice, it is quite an easy matter to count the spreading cards by threes instead of singly. The magician begins his counting as he tells the spectator to touch any card. As a result, the selected card will be well down in the pack.

If desired, a spectator may be allowed to simply peek at the corner of a card and the magician may slide the cards along further, allowing a choice of a second card. In this case he starts a second count or continues the first one. This is one of the best of all methods for determining the name of a selected card.

5. THE SLIDE OUT

While this form of card location is an old one, it is virtually unknown to the present day magician. We are describing it here,
with improvements, because it is a good, reliable method of con-

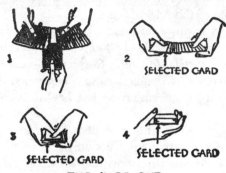

THE SLIDE OUT

(1) Selected card returned to the pack.
(2) The selected card drawn beneath the spread.
(3) The selected card at the bottom.
(4) Final stage of the sleight.

trolling a selected card. It serves the same purpose as Blackstone's
"Card Control."*

A certain amount of skill is necessary in the maneuver, as it
brings a selected card to the bottom of the pack. Nevertheless,
the movements are so natural and so simple that the method is by
no means difficult to learn.

Simply spread the pack between the hands and ask that a card
be selected. This card is returned to the center of the pack. Then
the left thumb draws a few cards to the left so that they cover the
selected one, as though making sure that it is lost in the middle of
the pack.

The spread, at this juncture, is quite wide. The pack has been
opened slightly to admit the return of the chosen card. The right

---

* Explained in Chapter VIII.

fingers, reaching beneath, slide the chosen card to the right. This is hidden by the cards which the left thumb has drawn over the chosen one. A short pull by the right fingers and the chosen card is clear of the pack—beneath it.

Now the pack is closed by bringing the hands together. It is no trick at all to let the selected card glide along the bottom as a free agent until it safely arrives on the bottom of the pack.

The maneuver may be repeated with another selected card— in fact as many cards may be used as required for the particular trick. Each one glides to the bottom. There they may be easily controlled.

Some readers may prefer this system to the Blackstone "Card Control," although the "Card Control" is unquestionably the superior method. It is interesting to compare the two, however, and good results may be obtained by alternating them.

In the "Slide Out," the magician may start to close the spread by pulling a few cards to the left; then he can begin to spread the cards again, telling the chooser to note that his card is actually in the center of the pack.

What the spectator sees is one of the cards which the left thumb drew over. Seeing only the back of the card, he takes it for granted that it is really his card. By diverting attention in this manner, the magician has an excuse for spreading the pack, which facilitates the sliding of the chosen card to the right. Then the pack is closed with a quick movement and the selected card goes to the bottom.

6. THE PUSH THROUGH

A card is selected from the pack. The magician holds the pack in his left hand and squares it so that all the cards are well together. He riffles the outer end of the pack so that the selected card may be inserted. This card projects—so the magician pushes it squarely into the pack.

This being done, he divides the pack into two heaps and proceeds with a dovetail shuffle. Everything is natural—in fact, the magician goes to great pains to show that there is no possible way for him to control the chosen card. Yet that is exactly what he does.

It's all in the "push." When the chosen card is inserted, the end projects, as has been mentioned. The magician pushes the card into the pack; in doing this, he strikes it rather forcibly. As a result, the card now projects from the inner end of the pack, where it cannot be seen by the spectators.

When the pack is divided into two heaps for the shuffle, the magician simply uses the projecting end of the selected card as

THE PUSH THROUGH

LEFT: Selected card returned and left projecting.
CENTER: The right hand strikes the card into the pack.
RIGHT: The chosen card projecting at the back.

a tab by which he can lift the upper portion. In shuffling, he lets this card fall first, thus placing it on the bottom of the pack.

If the cards are held slightly loose, the card will push through more readily. Remember that the strong part of this trick lies in its apparent fairness. It may be done deliberately, with good effect.

7 . THE PUSH BACK

A very neat form of location. Riffle the pack and allow a card to be selected. Raise the upper portion of the pack with the right hand so the card may be replaced upon the lower heap. Now comes the important move.

In setting the upper portion on the lower, bring the inner end down first. Let the tip of the right thumb rest upon the chosen card.

As the top portion of the pack is a trifle advanced, the hand is naturally drawn back so that the front edge of the pack will be even. Due to the pressure of the thumb, the chosen card moves backward as this action is performed.

The entire movement is covered by the upper heap. The front of the pack is tilted a trifle upward. The chosen card projects half an inch at the rear of the pack, but it is not observed.

The right hand squares the pack very carefully. With the pack squared and the chosen card presumably safely buried, the per-

THE PUSH BACK

How the right thumb pushes back the top card of the lower heap (the selected card) while placing the upper half of the pack in position.

former is ready to execute the dovetail shuffle. He can bring the selected card either to the top or bottom. For the bottom, he lifts its projecting end when he cuts the pack. For the top, he lifts all cards above the projection.

8. A NEAT LOCATION

A card having been selected, the magician squares the pack and holds it for the reception of the chosen card. He lifts up a large portion of the pack and invites the chooser to return his card. When this is done, the magician drops the rest of the pack on top.

In this natural procedure, he keeps the location of the chosen card. When he drops the upper portion, he lets it fall slightly toward himself, so the upper section projects inward. He immediately tilts the hand forward so the cards slide flush at the front.

But the card directly above the chosen one will not slide forward. It will remain, projecting inward. When the magician shuffles by the dovetail system, he uses this tab to lift off the upper half of the pack.

In shuffling, he lets the top card of the lower half be among the last to fall. It being the selected card, the result is that the performer brings the chosen card to the top of the pack where it is in just the position where he can use it.

9. THE FAN LOCATION

In this location, the pack is fanned or spread in the customary manner for a person to select a card. When it is replaced, the magician uses a very clever subterfuge. He holds the pack fanned

THE FAN LOCATION

Selected card inserted in the fan is pushed in almost flush. The squaring of the pack leaves it projecting.

rather closely, in the right hand. Thus it is impossible for the spectator to push the card entirely into the pack.

The magician may use his left hand to help—if the spectator pushes the card only about half way in, the performer can remark that it should go farther in, suiting the words with the action.

When the card is nearly in the pack, the magician turns slightly to the left and closes the fan by striking the left edge of the pack against the palm of his left hand. Even though he has pushed the chosen card well in, it will still project slightly. It forms a tab which can be easily located.

Note that at this point, the end of the pack from which the card projects is turned away from the spectators. The magician simply takes the pack and shuffles it in dovetail fashion. He catches the projecting card with his right thumb, separating the pack at that point. Letting the chosen card fall first, puts it on the bottom of the pack, from which position it is easily controlled.

10. A CARD DETECTION

This is a simple method of learning the name of a chosen card. It is particularly useful as it leaves the card in a very advantageous position—on the bottom of the pack, where the magician may learn the name of the card and reveal it as he sees fit.

Give the pack to a spectator. Tell him to shuffle it. Tell him to deal off any number of cards, faces up, one by one, making a heap —and to note the last card dealt. You turn your back while he does this. Suppose he deals eight and the last card is the five of spades. You do not know this and you tell him to replace the cards on the pack, remembering both the card and the number.

You turn away with the pack and work with it a few moments. Then you return it to the spectator, saying that you have mixed the cards but have not discovered the chosen one. Ask him to deal the same number that he dealt before—faces up—but not to remember any new card—to keep the name of the old card constantly in mind.

He does this while your back is turned and you ask him to replace the dealt cards upon the bottom of the pack. He is apt to notice that his card does not appear this time; that is natural, because you mixed the cards.

Again you take the cards and mix them, either by looking at them or by holding them behind your back. Then you discover his card—either by showing it to him on the bottom of the pack or by producing it in some clever manner.

How do you get the card? Simply enough. Suppose the spectator dealt twelve cards and put them on the top; then dealt twelve and put them on the bottom. The twelfth—chosen—card would naturally wind up on the bottom of the pack. That's the way you do the trick—but you do not work it so baldly.

When you first receive the pack, count off a number of cards from the bottom and put them on the top. That is done after the spectator's first deal. Remember the number of cards you use—say sixteen. After the second deal by the spectator, count off the same number of cards—sixteen in this case—but this time take them from the top of the pack and put them on the bottom. This has the same effect as the simple procedure described above. Perhaps, in reading it, you may think it won't work. But it does work—every time—and that is the beauty of it. Just follow the directions as specified and you will get the chosen card on the bottom of the pack where you want it.

11. THE PICK-UP HEAPS

This is a bold form of card location, but a deceptive one, if properly practiced. The magician divides the pack into three heaps— or allows someone else to do so. A card is selected and placed on one of the heaps. The magician drops that heap on another heap and drops the third heap on top. He appears to bury the selected card in the pack.

Actually, he is bringing the card to the top. It is done this way. Pick up the heap with the chosen card and drop that heap on another heap. As you do so, retain a few of the top cards between the tips of your thumb and fingers. In reaching for the odd heap, simply carry those extra cards along (the chosen card being on top of them) and let them fall on the final heap as you carry it to the pack.

This requires smartness of action, even though no special skill is necessary. There is an important point that adds much. If you intend to use your right hand, make sure that the spectators are mostly to your right. Your hand, tilting slightly in their direction, covers the carried cards very effectively.

If the spectators are on your left, use the left hand to execute the three-heap pick-up.

12. SURPASSO

This is the title of a remarkable card detection that is one of the newest and best ideas in card conjuring. It approaches the impossible when well performed; and the trick is not difficult, although it requires close attention to detail.

Anyone removes a pack of cards from its case and gives the pack a shuffle. Then the person selects a card and puts it face down in the case. Following the magician's instructions, the per-

LEFT: Selected card is first placed in case.
CENTER: Then the pack itself is inserted.
RIGHT: Selected card discovered projecting.

son then inserts the pack, seeing to it that the selected card is buried amongst the others. This is accomplished by making a little space in the pack to receive the chosen card.

The magician takes the case as the spectator closes it and retires to the opposite side of the room. He looks at the case; then at the spectator. He removes the cards from the case, runs through the pack and produces the selected card!

The secret is a simple one. Using the usual style flap case, the pack, when pushed in, has a tendency to shove the single card further down. To make sure of this, the magician should approach and take the pack just as soon as the spectator has the pack well in. If the pack fits the case rather tightly, so much the better.

Across the room, the magician inverts the case and taps the flap end against his hand. This evens the pack a bit. When he removes the pack from the case, the magician grips it firmly and he will discover one card projecting a fraction of an inch from the lower end. That card is the selected card. He takes it from the pack.

The use of the case makes the trick good, because no one can see the projecting card.

13. AN EASY FORCE

This idea has many uses. It is explained here in a simple and effective form. The magician lays a pack on the table. He writes something on a sheet of paper. He asks someone to cut the pack at any point. The paper is laid between the two portions.

Known card on bottom of pack. Top half removed; lower half placed on it. Bottom card arrives at the center, ready for selection.

When the upper half of the pack is lifted, the spectators are asked to note the card on its face—suppose it is the queen of clubs. The paper is unfolded. It bears the name "queen of clubs."

This is accomplished by simply noting the bottom card of the pack after a shuffle. That is the name which the magician writes on the sheet of paper. It does not matter where the pack is cut. The magician simply picks up the lower half of the pack and completes the cut by dropping it on the top half—but he inserts the sheet of paper as he does so.

Thus it is the bottom card—the known card—which comes on top of the sheet of paper. But the method is so natural and so subtle that persons will be positive the magician put the paper at an unknown spot near the center of the pack.

For ordinary forcing or location purposes, the magician may note secretly the top card of the pack; then ask someone to cut the cards and to complete the cut by leaving the upper portion at an angle. Then a spectator is allowed to look at the card immediately below the break. This is the card that the wizard knows;

but people will not realize it. That card can be discovered later
—after a shuffle.

14. THE JOKER FORCE

This is by no means a new idea; but it is a very useful one. It
enables the magician to learn the name of a card before the card
is drawn.

It begins after a borrowed pack has been shuffled. The magician
takes the pack, turns the bottom card toward himself and remarks
that he must remove the joker. He spreads the cards from the
bottom; when he reaches the joker, he discards it and lays the
pack face down upon the table.

The pack is now cut into three heaps. Choice is given of one.
The top card of the heap is noted by a spectator. Strange though
it may seem, the magician knows that card and no matter how
often the pack may be shuffled he can always look through and
find it.

The trick begins with the removal of the joker. As he runs
through the bottom cards of the pack, in his search for the joker,
the magician slyly slides the top card a trifle to the left—just far
enough so he can see its index corner. After removing the joker,
he squares the pack and divides it into three heaps. He lifts off
two-thirds of the face-down pack and places the large upper portion to the right of the lower. He then lifts half of the upper portion
and puts it between the two heaps.

This tricky cut is seldom noticed. It puts the top of the pack in
the middle of the heaps, although one would normally suppose
the top portion was at the right.

When the magician asks that a heap be chosen, the spectator
usually obliges by taking the center one. He is told to look at the
top card of the heap—the very card that the magician knows.

Suppose that the center heap is not chosen? Very well. The
magician tells the person who takes an end heap to remove it.
Then he remarks that there are two heaps left. One must be
eliminated. Which does the person want?

If the desired heap is touched, the magician says: "You want that one? Well, that eliminates this one." If the wrong heap is indicated, the magician's response is: "So that's the one you want eliminated. Well, that leaves this one."

An interesting trick performed by the joker force is to ascribe wonderful powers to the joker itself—a good excuse for removing it from the pack. When the center heap is chosen (whether the spectator wants it or not!) the magician tells the chooser to push the top card off the heap and on to the table.

Then the card is touched with the joker. The magician pretends to hold conversation with the joker. It tells him the name of the card and the magician announces that name. To prove the joker was correct, he uses the joker to flip the single card face up on the table and the statement is seen to be true.

15. THE FORCE LOCATION

This form of card location involves a simple type of card force. It is designed to work to the performer's advantage whether or not the right card is actually selected by the spectator.

Briefly, the magician spreads the pack and asks that a card be selected. This card is removed and replaced in the pack, which is fairly closed. The magician later discovers or names the selected card.

The first thing the magician does is to note the bottom card of the pack. He draws off the lower portion and transfers it to the top, keeping the two sections slightly apart so that he can handle the known card.

In spreading the pack, he pushes this card a trifle forward so that it projects more than the others and is the logical card which the average person would select. If that card is taken, well and good. Everything is as the magician wishes it.

Now suppose the known card is not selected. In most instances the chooser will pick a card quite close to it. The magician can visually count to the card that the spectator draws. It may, for example, be three cards below the known one—or five cards above. It may often be the card next to the known one.

Under such circumstances, the magician says to the spectator:

"Don't remove the card from the pack—just look at its corner." This enables the magician to close tho pack, holding the chosen card at its relative position from the known one. Needless to say, the chosen card may be easily discovered by looking for the known card and counting to it. The pack is not shuffled—unless a false method is used.

Should the spectator pick a card well away from the card which the magician desired to force, another procedure is available. The performer lets the spectator take the card clear of the deck. When it is about to be replaced, the wizard raises the pack at the known card, forming a space for the return of the selected one.

This brings the chosen card next to the known card and the matter of locating the chosen card is simplified. In a great percentage of cases, the known card will be the one selected and in such instances, this additional action is not necessary.

Nevertheless, it gives the magician an excellent way of avoiding the embarrassment that follows the selection of the wrong card when a force is attempted. The old style procedure was to do another trick when the force missed; but it is much more satisfactory to utilize the forcing card as a locator when the emergency calls for it.

16. BEHIND THE BACK

This is an excellent method for forcing a card. The magician holds a shuffled pack behind his back. He lets a person lift off some cards. The magician asks that the next card be noted. This is done. The card is then replaced; the pack is shuffled by the audience. Nevertheless, the magician knows the name of the card.

He manages this by removing the card from the pack *before* he begins the trick. If the magician simply wants to know the name of any card that the audience may take, he removes any card and notes its identity. If he wants a certain card taken, he removes that card from the pack. The magician tucks this card beneath his belt, behind his back, the face of the card being outward.

Tricks are performed while that card is missing from the pack, no one realizing that it is absent. When the performer wishes to have the card selected, he turns his back and tells someone to put the pack face down in his left hand; then to lift a number of cards.

As soon as the cards are raised, the magician swings toward the spectator, with some pertinent remark, such as: "You took off some cards, didn't you?" This hides the left hand momentarily. Raising the hand to his belt, the magician draws away the hidden card so that it lies on top of the cards that are in his left hand.

Turning away again, the magician extends his left hand behind his back and asks the spectator to look at the next card—that is, the card now on top of the left hand packet. Inasmuch as it is totally impossible for the magician to have seen the card, there is no suspicion. This card is noted; then the pack is shuffled.

In brief, the magician has simply added his held-out card in such a way that it is logically selected and he can proceed with the trick without danger of detection.

This method can be used in a different way, however. When the spectator lifts a bunch of cards, the magician can turn and tell him to glance at the bottom card of the group he has taken. While the spectator is doing so, the magician adds the extra card. Turning his back, he asks that the spectator's group be replaced. This is done. The chosen card is now directly above the card that the performer knows. Hence the discovery of the selected card is not a difficult matter.

In this method, the pack should be cut a few times behind the magician's back—not shuffled. This is merely a variation of the forcing idea and is mentioned because it has occasional use.

17. THE GLIMPSE

This maneuver is aptly named, because in practice, the magician glimpses the index corner of a card after it has been returned to the pack. Thus learning the name of the card, he can allow the pack to be shuffled, yet can find it when he wants it.

First Method: Simply insert the left little finger beneath the card after it has been returned to the pack. The finger is at the right, inner corner. Raise the upper portion of the pack slightly and shift it a trifle to the left. At the same time bring the left edge of the pack straight up. Note the index corner with a downward glance and immediately close the pack, removing the little finger from between the two portions.

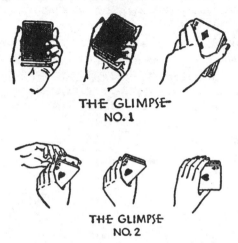

THE GLIMPSE
NO. 1

THE GLIMPSE
NO. 2

The methods of glimpsing a card in the center of the pack are depicted here.

Second Method: Riffle the front edge of the pack and ask a person to insert his finger. When he does so, tell him to note the card above his finger. Let the rest of the pack fall with a quick riffle, but press the ball of your left forefinger against the outer right corner so a space remains there.

The left thumb, on top of the pack, pushes the upper portion a trifle to the right as the left hand turns the pack face up, toward yourself. This gives you a glimpse of the selected card and the right hand immediately takes the pack, bottom up, closing the space. The right hand offers the pack to a spectator for shuffling.

Third Method: This is for sighting the top card of the pack, after the cards have been shuffled. It is useful in certain tricks. Hold the pack in the left hand. The fingers are beneath; the thumb is across the top.

During a gesture of the left hand, the thumb pushes the top card a fraction of an inch to the right and a trifle forward. The left hand turns the end of the pack almost straight up and the index corner of the top card is sighted.

A good finish to this movement is to square the pack by tapping it upon the table—a logical excuse for the movement of the pack.

Another way of utilizing this glimpse is to perform it while transferring the pack from the left hand to the right. The left hand turns the pack almost face upward, the thumb pushing the top card out. The fingers of the right hand cover the tell-tale corner and the right hand grips the pack, fingers below, thumb above, turning the pack face down.

Chapter III

CARD DISCOVERIES

After a card has been selected and replaced in the pack, the performer naturally discovers it in order to complete the trick which he is exhibiting.

The simplest form of card discovery is to pick the card out of the pack. That is effective when the spectators are sure that the magician has no way of finding the card. To discover one card out of a possible fifty-two is a good trick in itself.

But to get effective results in card magic, the performer should utilize various surprising methods of producing a chosen card after it has been lost in the pack. Such methods are known as card discoveries.

This section includes a list of effective discoveries following the selection of a card. The reader may choose those which interest him the most and by using them in connection with locations, he will be able to form a most surprising repertoire.

The usual steps before a card discovery are: the selection of a card; its replacement; its control or location by a method known to the magician; the shuffling of the pack (by false shuffles or cuts). Then the stage is set for the surprising appearance of the selected card.

1. THE KNOCK OUT

An effective conclusion to a card trick. This method is well-known, but is mentioned here because it is always good and also because of its variations. Note the points of difference in the methods. The magician holds the pack in his left hand. He strikes it with his right or allows a spectator to perform that action. The result: the only card that remains in the magician's hand is the one that was selected beforehand by a spectator.

First Method: The selected card is brought to the bottom of the pack. Hold the pack firmly in the left hand, fingers beneath and thumb on top. Hold it at one corner. The pack is face down. When the cards are struck, all are knocked from the hand except the bottom (selected) card.

Second Method: This time the selected card is brought to the top of the pack, which is held face up. The blow works the same, but the selected card is face up, staring at the spectators. This is a better effect.

Third Method: The card is brought to the top. The pack is held face downward. The spectator is asked to strike the pack *upward*. As a result, cards are scattered everywhere. The magician's hand goes upward with the blow so that only the selected card remains, facing the spectators.

2. CARD FROM THE POCKET

This is an old method of discovering a selected card; but it is given here with a puzzling addition. The pack is placed in the performer's inside pocket. Someone is told to reach in and draw out a card. He does so—and he brings out the selected card!

The answer is that the selected card is on top of the pack. By hurrying the person, the magician causes him to draw off the top card—the only one which he can easily and naturally grasp. The top of the pack is outward in the pocket.

Now for the improvement. Two selected cards. The magician shuffles the pack and puts it in his pocket. Reaching in, he draws out one of the selected cards.

Then, as an added feature, he takes the pack from his pocket and lets anyone shuffle it. Back it goes in the pocket. A spectator is told to seize a card from the pack. He does so—out comes the second selected card!

How does the magician get around the shuffle? Simply enough. He has both selected cards on top. He draws out one himself. When he brings out the pack to be shuffled, he leaves the other selected card in his pocket. It goes on top of the pack again, when the magician replaces the pack. That's why the grabbing spectator gets it.

3. ANY NUMBER

Here we make a chosen card appear at any number in the pack after the pack has been shuffled. Suppose nine is the number given. The chosen card is on top of the pack, brought there by the magician. He counts off nine cards one by one—this count reversed their order. He shows the ninth card. It is not the chosen one. So the performer puts the nine cards back on the pack.

He recalls that he forgot the magic riffle. So he riffles the pack and again counts to nine. Due to the reversed order, the chosen card shows up at the required number—in this instance, just nine cards from the top of the pack.

Now for an improvement on the old idea. Suppose nine is given, with the chosen card on top. Count off eight (reversing their order). Drop the ninth on the table and ask the person to look at it. While attention is directed there, the eight cards are brought back to the pack by the right hand. The right fingers push the chosen card forward. The left hand, tilting to the right, allows the card to come face up on the rest of the pack; rather, the left hand puts the pack face down on the chosen card. Swinging to its normal position, the left hand receives the other cards on top of the pack, as they should be.

The performer does this automatically. It is all finished by the time the spectator has discovered that the ninth card is not the one he selected. So the magician puts that card on top of the pack and resorts to his magic riffle.

Then comes the surprise. Counting slowly to nine, the magician reveals the chosen card at the desired number and furthermore the chosen card is face up—just a little token of the potency of the wizard's riffle!

One important fact should be noted—for this trick and all others that involve reversed cards. Only perform such effects with packs that have a white margin on the backs. Otherwise, there will be difficulty. Most good packs have the required white margins.

Any slight unevenness of the pack will not betray a reversed card, if white margins are used. But with packs that have a design running solid to the border, reversed card tricks should be avoided.

4. A REVERSED CARD

A card having been selected and returned to the pack, the magician starts a search for it. He finds a card and lays it face upward on top of the pack.

"That's your card, isn't it?" he asks.

"No," is the reply.

"What!" exclaims the mystifier. "Not the six of spades? I'll have to try again."

He removes the seven of diamonds and thrusts it back into the pack, which he shuffles. Then he turns the pack face downward and spreads it. One card appears face up. It proves to be the card selected.

The Method: The magician easily finds the chosen card by whatever system he chooses to use. But he draws it from the pack in back of the six of spades—that is, he holds the two cards as one and instantly lays them face upward on top of the pack.

Finding that the six of spades is not correct, the magician tilts the pack upward so that only the faces of cards can be seen. He takes the six of spades from the top of the pack and puts it properly among the other cards.

But this time, he manages the six of spades alone—leaving the chosen card face up on top of the pack. A short easy shuffle—keeping the faces of the cards toward the spectators—puts the chosen card in the midst of the pack—face up, ready for the finish.

5. ONE REVERSED CARD

An easy reversed card trick, depending upon one simple move which can be made slowly without fear of detection. A chosen card is brought to the top of the pack. The magician shuffles

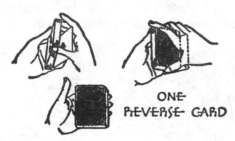

ONE
REVERSE CARD

Movements of shifting the top card of the pack so it lies face up on the bottom.

with the faces of the cards toward the spectators and he keeps the chosen card on top of the pack.

Completing the shuffle, he grips the top card with the fingers of his left hand. At the same time, the right hand (thumb at one end, fingers at the other) lifts the pack a trifle upward and forward and turns it face down.

The left hand goes flat as the pack is turned, so the magician simply lays the pack on that single, face-up card. All that is now necessary is to cut the pack; then spread it on the table. The chosen card will be seen face up in the midst of the face-down cards.

6. THREE REVERSED CARDS

This is a very bewildering card trick. The magician apparently causes three selected cards to reverse themselves so they lie faces up at different parts of the pack.

The first card selected is brought to the top of the pack. The magician places it face up on the bottom (as described in the preceding "One Reversed Card" trick). He leaves the card on the bottom.

Now he spreads the pack (watching the bottom card) and has two more cards taken, by persons well apart. Squaring the pack he walks from person three to person two. As he does so, he turns the pack over in his left hand, so the single card is face up on bottom. He tells person two to insert his card at any spot, calling

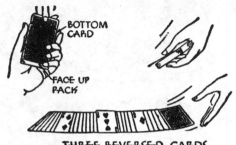

THREE REVERSED CARDS

UPPER LEFT: How the pack is held face up, with one selected card inverted upon it. Second card is being inserted.

UPPER RIGHT: Third selected card projecting on the top of pack.

BOTTOM: The result—three cards, faces up.

attention to the fact that the pack is squared so the card's position cannot be noted. The card goes in face down. Thus, like the card on the bottom, it is inverted or reversed.

Going back to person three, the magician, with a swing of his hand, brings the real top of the pack uppermost again. He lifts a few cards off with his right hand and transfers them to the bottom, saying: "When I cut like this, put your card on."

Lifting a few more, the magician allows the placement of the third chosen card. He drops the right hand cards upon it and immediately brings the card to the top of the pack.*

The result now is that one chosen card is on top of the pack. The others are reversed but buried. The magician holds the pack across his right hand, with the thumb on top. He pushes the top

* The "Revolving Pass" is useful at this point.

card slightly forward and lets the pack slide along the table—or better, along the floor.

This maneuver, if properly done, causes the top card to turn over on the pack, due to the air pressure. It travels along with the pack and seems to bob out from some unexpected spot. At the same time, the spreading pack reveals the other two chosen cards, each lying face up amidst the pack.

It looks like a triple reverse and the fact that the cards are far apart has a marked effect upon those who witness it. This trick should be carefully rehearsed, as it contains many points that must be remembered, even though it has been simplified in method so that any performer of ordinary ability can demonstrate it without recourse to unusual dexterity.

7. OUT OF THE HAT

This is a great finish for a card trick. Cards are selected and replaced in the pack, which is shuffled. The magician handles the deck a while; then spies a felt hat, into which he drops the pack. He holds the hat with the brim upward. He flips the crown of the hat with his forefinger. Out come the selected cards, sailing toward the ceiling!

There is no great difficulty in this trick. It may be performed with one or more selected cards. They are brought to the top of the pack or to the bottom. In either instance, the magician is set for the hat trick. When he drops the pack into the hat, he keeps the opening of the hat toward himself. He lets the pack go into one section of the hat; but he retains the selected cards and slides them into the other section of the hat.

Holding the hat above the spectators' line of vision, the magician makes a sharp flip against the crown of the hat. But he chooses the side where the selected cards are located. The force of the flip causes the cards to fly out of the hat in a most mysterious fashion. The hat is immediately tilted forward and the rest of the pack is allowed to slide out on the table.

8. BLACKSTONE'S CUT TRICK

This is one of the finest of all card discoveries. Two cards are selected by the audience. The magician shuffles the pack after the cards are returned. He riffles the end of the pack and asks a third person to insert another card, face upward, at any point in the pack.

This is done. The third person retains his hold on the face-up card. The magician withdraws the entire pack, with the exception of two cards—the one above the inserted card and the one below.

BLACKSTONE'S CUT TRICK

(1) Pack with one chosen card on top; other on bottom.
(2) Pack cut. Little finger retains the break.
(3) Riffling for the face-up insertion of an odd card.
(4) Drawing off from the break, showing face-up card.
(5) Top half replaced upon the lower.
(6) Pack spread to find inserted card between chosen ones.

Holding these three cards, the conjuror calls for the names of the selected cards. The names given, he turns over the three cards in his hand. This reveals the two selected cards! The spectator has thrust his face-up card between them!

The Secret: The two selected cards are first received in the pack and one is brought to the top; the other to the bottom. This is done by a card location system and is aided by false shuffles.

Now the magician cuts the pack by drawing off some of the bottom cards, to the rear, with his right hand. He puts the lower half on the upper half. This brings the selected cards together, but the left little finger holds a space between them. The cut should be made so that the two cards are fairly near the bottom of the pack as it now stands.

Riffling the pack at the outer end (with the right fingers) the magician invites the insertion of the odd face-up card. If it happens to go in the space between the two selected cards, well and good. But the magician is riffling rapidly to reach that space and the card often goes in above it.

With his right hand, the magician simply grips the upper portion of the pack (all cards above the break held by the left little finger). His right thumb is below; fingers above. He draws back the entire portion of the pack until it is free of the face-up card which the spectator is holding. Then he slaps that portion down upon the face-up card.

This movement is natural, sure and undetectable. It brings one chosen card directly above the inserted card; the other directly beneath. The rest of the pack is spread out and drawn away, leaving only the three cards—two selected and one inserted between them.

The same trick can be performed with the aid of a knife, which is inserted instead of a face-up card. The procedure is exactly the same, the knife blade serving as the indicator in this instance.

9. CARD IN CIGAR BOX

A great trick. A chosen card is replaced in the pack, which the magician shuffles. The wizard then empties some cigars from an ordinary cigar box. He shows the box empty. He closes it and lays the pack on it. A mystic pass; the box is opened—the card is found therein.

The card actually goes into the cigar box—but before the spectators suppose. The magician gets it to the top of the pack. He palms it off and in going to the cigar box, keeps the card in readiness. The cigars are emptied—in drops the card from the wizard's palm.

The regulation cigar box is lined with paper—and the paper overlaps along the bottom. When the magician drops the card in the box, his hands are free and as he picks up the box to show it to the spectators, he tilts it so the selected card slides under the overlapping paper.

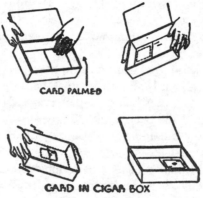

The diagrams illustrate the routine of the card in the cigar box.

This enables him to show the box absolutely empty and to let the spectators close the box. When the box is shut, the magician sets it on the table, tilting it as he does so. The card drops from its hiding place. It is then in the box, ready for its mysterious appearance.

By using a duplicate card, the magician can have one already hidden in the box. He must then force that card upon the audience and later remove it from the pack.

10. CARD ELIMINATION

A card having been selected and returned to the pack, the magician offers to determine its identity by a process of elimination.

He takes eight cards and holds them faces down. Showing each card, he deals four on the table. None is the selected one. He deals two of these on the table. Neither is the one chosen. Then one card is left; it proves to be the chosen card.

This trick depends upon the sleight called the "glide."* The selected card is actually among the eight—which the magician does not show. The card is second from the bottom.

Here is the procedure. Holding the cards faces down, the magician shows the bottom card and asks if it is the chosen one. The spectator says that it is not. So the magician apparently deals it face down on the table. Actually he makes use of the "glide" and the chosen card is the one dealt.

The performer says he will put the next card back in the pack, eliminating it. So he draws off the bottom card of those in the little packet and replaces it on the pack without showing it. He shows the next card, however, and actually deals it face down. Then another on the pack, alternating thus, so there are four cards faces down on the table—the chosen card among them.

The magician gathers the four cards and sees to it that the selected card is again second from the bottom. He shows the bottom card and apparently deals it. Actually the chosen card is dealt —the "glide" again. The bottom card is then replaced, unshown, upon the pack. The next card is shown and dealt face down. The fourth goes into the pack.

The elimination has left only two cards—neither of which is supposed to be the chosen one. The spectators are wondering what the magician is about. He asks a person to place a hand on either card. Suppose the person touches the chosen card. The magician picks up the other card, shows its face and says: "Of course this is not your card," and replaces it in the pack. That leaves only one card. Turned up, it proves to be the chosen one.

Of course there is a possibility that the spectator will decide to touch the card which the magician wishes to eliminate. That makes no difference. He is simply told to turn up the card and look at it—not the chosen card, of course. It is put in the pack. That leaves just one card—which proves to be the chosen one.

Artfully done, this trick is surprising at the finish, because the

* Explained in Section One.

performer seems to be dealing with cards other than the chosen one. The appearance of the selected card comes as a real bit of amazement. The trick must be done neatly—but very little skill is needed.

Chapter IV

SPELLING TRICKS

The original spelling tricks were simply "spelling bees" performed with a set of cards. Then came the use of the spelling idea for the discovery of a chosen card.

There are now various good tricks which involve the spelling of a chosen card and this section includes the best of them. It logically follows card discoveries as some of the spellers are discoveries in themselves.

Others form complete tricks, from beginning to end, including the location of the card which is to be spelled. This section represents the latest development in up-to-date card magic.

The spelling trick is so novel that it invariably calls for a repetition; hence the various methods given will be useful as they enable the magician to employ the spelling in different ways.

The novel application of the spelling principle, revealing a selected card by dealing with each letter of the name, will be appreciated fully through a careful perusal of the tricks in this section. They show how the spelling method simplifies certain tricks instead of complicating them.

1. SIMPLICITY SPELLER

This begins like the usual card trick. The magician takes a pack of cards and spreads it between his hands, running the cards from left to right. He asks a person to select a card and to remove it from the pack. That having been done, the magician lifts some cards so that the chosen one may be replaced.

Riffling the pack, the magician states that he will make the card choose its own position. He asks the spectator to name the card. We will suppose that it is the five of hearts. The magician commences to deal the cards, spelling: "F-I-V-E-O-F-H-E-A-R-T-S—" a letter for each card. With the final "S," he turns up the card. It proves to be the five of hearts.

The important method of the trick is quite simple. In running the cards from the left hand to the right, the magician counts them. He does not give anyone a chance to take a card until he has run eleven cards along the fan. He pushes the cards more slowly after the eleventh, keeping a slight space between the eleventh card and the twelfth.

When a card is removed, the magician invites its replacement, by lifting the eleven cards at the top of the pack. As a result, the selected card takes the position of number twelve.

Now it is not at all difficult to spell to the chosen card after it is named. Simply count the letters to oneself. If the card is spelled with eleven letters, spell it and turn up the twelfth. If twelve letters, end the spelling on the twelfth. With thirteen letters, leave out the word "O-F." Example: queen of hearts. Spell: "Q-U-E-E-N-H-E-A-R-T-S" and turn up the next card. With fourteen letters, leave out the word "O-F" and turn up the card with the final letter of the spelling.

There remain only two possibilities: ten-letter cards and fifteen-letter cards. These are a minority. With a ten-letter card, the magician turns the top card of the pack face up and appears surprised because it is not the chosen card. He lays that card aside; thinks a moment; then brightens and spells the name of the card, turning up the card after the last letter.

With a fifteen-letter card, the magician spells very slowly. He says (for example): "Your card was the seven of diamonds? I shall spell 'S-E-V-E-N.' The suit? A diamond? Very well: 'D-I-A-M-O-N-D.'"

He turns up the card on the final "D" and reveals it as the seven of diamonds. Thus by a little ingenuity, the chosen card can be spelled every time. This is one of the most practical and effective versions of the spelling trick. It requires some amount of rehearsal in order to be presented convincingly, but the actual skill involved is negligible.

2. SPREAD-OUT SPELLER

There is a certain similarity between this effect and the trick we have called the "Simplicity Speller." The reader should compare the two methods, for a reason which will be mentioned later.

A shuffled pack is spread along the table. A card is chosen from any spot. Only the person selecting it sees it. The card is re-

SPREAD OUT SPELLER

Noting thirteen cards above selected one. Making break at that point. Shifting extra cards to bottom. Also the final position.

placed from where it was taken. The performer picks up the pack and requests the name of the card. He spells the name, dealing a card with each letter. The spelling ends by the turning up of the chosen card.

It is all a matter of careful counting. The pack is spread clear along the table. As soon as the spectator touches a card, the magician counts along the line to a spot thirteen cards above the chosen one (beginning the count with the touched card).

As the spectator replaces the card he took, the magician still keeps his eye upon the place to which he has counted. He has spread the cards from left to right. Sliding them up with his left hand, he holds a break with his left thumb when he reaches the spot to which he has counted. The right hand simply transfers all

cards above the break, putting them on the bottom of the pack.
Thus the chosen card is thirteen from the top. The wizard asks
its name and spells in such a manner that he ends with the chosen
card.

For instance, if the card has only ten letters, he adds the word
"T-H-E" before it. Example: "T-H-E-A-C-E-O-F-C-L-U-B-S."
With eleven letters, he removes the top card from the pack, strikes
the pack with it, and thrusts the card into the pack at the center.
This by-play disposes of an odd card. It leaves only twelve to deal.
The magician spells with eleven cards and turns up the *next* card.

Twelve letters is a simple spelling, turning up the next card;
thirteen letters spell right to the card itself. With fourteen letters,
eliminate the word "O-F" and turn up the card after the spelling.
With fifteen letters, eliminate "O-F" and turn up on the final letter.

There is another method of gathering up the cards from the
table—simply a variation of the one described. Sweep them up
with the right hand until the desired spot is reached. Then transfer those cards to the left hand and use them as a lever to gather
up the cards from left to right. This puts the chosen card thirteen
from the top.

In comparing this method with the "Simplicity Speller," note
that here the chosen card is set at thirteen; with the other method,
it is set at twelve. There is no reason why the reader should not
adopt one standard for both methods. Either keep the chosen card
twelve from the top or put it thirteen from the top and act accordingly. Both systems are explained here, to show how flexible
the spelling can be.

3. FOUR HEAP SPELLER

This is one of the most interesting versions of the spelling trick.
It can be demonstrated with an ease of action that defies detection. It requires boldness more than skill.

A spectator is asked to shuffle a pack of cards and to cut it in
half. He is then requested to cut each half into two equal portions.
The result: four heaps.

He is told to look at the top card of any heap and to place it on any other heap. This done, the magician gathers the heaps, burying the chosen card in the pack.

The card is named. The magician proceeds to deal cards off, faces upward, spelling a letter as he deals each card. "F-O-U-R-O-F-H-E-A-R-T-S—" he spells and on the letter "S" he is holding the four of hearts!

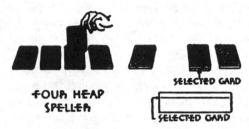

LEFT: Division of pack in four equal heaps.
RIGHT: One heap placed on selected card. Final position before the spelling.

It so happens that the separation of the pack into four approximately equal heaps puts about thirteen cards in each heap. Thus, when a card is selected from the top of a heap, it is quite possible to put that card just about thirteen from the top when the heaps are gathered. Merely drop a single heap upon the chosen card.

Let us suppose, by way of example, that the chosen card is just about thirteen from the top of the pack—the exact location being unknown. When the cards are spelled, they are dropped faces up, each letter being given just before the card is tilted into view.

The count, or spelling, is rapid at first, but it slows appreciably. "F-O-U-R-O-F-D-I---A--M--O--N--D---"

On the final "D" we have reached the zone of the selected card. If it turns up on the letter "D," the magician smiles and holds the card out for all to see. He has completed the spelling! If it does not show up, he drops the card; then, he deals another card saying "S." This is likely to be the chosen card—if so, the trick is done. If it is not the chosen card, he simply drops it and deals off the *next* card very decisively, turning it up to reveal it as the four of diamonds.

In brief, the magician has *three chances* of hitting the chosen card and any one will bring the trick to a successful finish.

It is wise, in picking up the heaps, to drop a slightly under-sized heap on the chosen card. The heaps should be almost equal. They seldom are exact, however. It is advisable to put *ten* or *eleven* cards on top, in preference to a larger number.

The magician must act carefully when he begins to spell. With any ten-letter card, such as the ace, two, six, nine of clubs, he does best to spell with the word "T-H-E" leading off, giving the particular card a thirteen valuation. With any fifteen-letter card, such as the three, seven, eight, queen of diamonds, he should spell simply the value and the suit, eliminating the word "O-F."

By following this plan, the performer is almost certain of striking the chosen card on one of his three all-important chances. With a reasonable amount of rehearsal, the trick becomes almost certain of success. The performer may, if he wishes, form the four heaps himself, thus increasing the chances of exactness.

The four heap speller may be extended by having two cards selected and placing the heap with one selected card upon the heap that has the other. Then a heap on top of both. This leaves everything set to spell to the second card after the discovery of the first. This additional effect should only be utilized when the heaps are almost identical in size, as it is then possible to depend upon the number thirteen.

There is another way of using the four heap idea. Tell a person to cut the pack in half; then lift half of the top portion and glance at a card, replacing the cards just as they were. Then the pack is taken by the magician who spells to the chosen card. This is simply an artifice that causes the spectator to look at either the thirteenth card or a card about thirteen from the top of the pack. The dealing and spelling are the same as in the four heap method.

4. EASY SPELLING TRICK

This is simply a new form of an old card-counting trick. Nevertheless, it makes a good speller. The effect is that a chosen card is returned to the pack. The magician asks its name. He spells it, a card being dealt for each letter. He turns up the last card of the deal. It is not the chosen card.

Perplexed, the wizard recalls that he forgot to rifflo the pack. He does so. More than that, he puts the pack in the hands of the person who chose the card and lets him do the spelling. This time it arrives on the chosen card.

The chosen card is on the top of the pack when the first spelling begins. It is brought there by whatever method the performer prefers. In spelling, the performer peels off the cards one by one, holding each face down. He draws the second card on to the first; the third on to the second and so on.

Of course the spelling does not work; but when the dealt off cards are put back on the top, it is all set, for the chosen card is now the bottom of the dealt group instead of the top. The performer has reversed their order in spelling so when the spectator goes over the ground, his spelling ends upon the selected card.

5. THE MENTAL SPELLER

The magician takes a pack of cards and opens it some distance from the top, spreading a series of cards so that they come into view when the front of the pack is fanned before a spectator's eyes.

The onlooker is told to make a mental selection of any card. The wizard closes the pack and riffles it. He asks the name of the card. Whatever it may be, the magician promptly spells to the chosen card. He may then repeat the trick with another person.

The secret lies in the special arrangement of seven cards. It will be noted that each of these cards is spelled with a different number of letters; the sixth and seventh are the same, but there is a simple way of giving an extra value to the seventh.

S-I-X-O-F-C-L-U-B-S .... 10 letters
A-C-E-O-F-H-E-A-R-T-S .... 11 letters
Q-U-E-E-N-O-F-C-L-U-B-S .... 12 letters
E-I-G-H-T-O-F-S-P-A-D-E-S .... 13 letters

K-I-N-G-O-F-D-I-A-M-O-N-D-S ....14 letters
S-E-V-E-N-O-F-D-I-A-M-O-N-D-S ....15 letters
T-H-R-E-E-O-F-D-I-A-M-O-N-D-S* ....16 letters

The asterisk (*) indicates that a card is turned up *after* the spelling is completed. In the other instances, the spelling ends with the final letter in the name of the card.

Based on this simple formula, the magician is ready to mystify.

He arranges his seven pet cards and places nine indifferent cards upon them. The entire group goes on top of the deck. Performing, the magician casually counts nine cards down and spreads the pack at that point, so when he turns the faces toward the audience, only seven cards are in view—the seven arranged cards.

It makes no difference which one is selected. The magician simply spells to it. Ten spelled letters arrive on the six of clubs; eleven on the ace of hearts; and so on—the only special instance being the three of diamonds. If it is the chosen card, the magician spells his deal and turns up the next card after he has completed.

Of course the trick can be repeated. This can be done with the same setup. It is an excellent idea, however, to have another group of cards arranged. Place nine indifferent cards under the three of diamonds; then set: ten of clubs, two of spades, seven of clubs, queen of hearts, jack of diamonds, three of diamonds, queen of diamonds.

After spelling to the chosen card of the first group, casually drop those cards aside; also the few more that may remain in the group. Again bunch nine cards at the top of the pack and give selection of the second setup.

It is merely a repetition of the trick. When only one group is being used, any borrowed pack may be quickly arranged as there are various options: ace of spades will answer for ten of hearts; three of spades for eight of spades, etc.

This cannot be regarded as a trick with a prearranged pack because the actual preparation is such a simple matter and may often be done in the course of other tricks. Even if the magician should pick his own cards, and someone comment upon the fact, he can easily explain it as a problem of psychology, stating that he will cause a person to pick a certain card, even against his will.

The "Mental Speller" is quite different from most of the other spelling effects and forms an excellent variation that will create much favorable comment among those who witness its performance.

6. THE PROGRESSIVE SPELLER

This form of the spelling trick requires some arrangement of the cards. That, however, should not detract from the effect, especially when the trick is presented at a small gathering where the magician appears as a special performer.

Several persons are handed packets of cards. Each is told to remember one card. The magician gathers each packet. He places all on the pack. He calls upon one spectator to name his card. This done, the magician spells to the card exactly. The effect is repeated with each of the other persons.

We have stated that "several" persons are handed "packets" of cards. In practice, the number of persons is exactly four; and there are just five cards in each heap. These cards are arranged progressively for spelling, as in the "Mental Speller."

Group 1: jack of clubs, four of hearts, queen of spades, five of diamonds, eight of diamonds.

Group 2: ten of hearts, eight of clubs, seven of spades, jack of diamonds, seven of diamonds.

Group 3: two of spades, queen of clubs, ten of diamonds, king of diamonds, three of diamonds.

Group 4: ace of hearts, king of spades, eight of hearts, four of diamonds, queen of diamonds.

These heaps are on top of the pack. If the magician indulges in cuts or shuffles before dealing, he must use false ones that do not disturb the order of the twenty cards. He goes to four different persons, dealing five to each in turn. He fans the cards for a selection and has the person hold his cards just as given to him—face down, after the mental selection.

Finishing with the four persons, the magician casually counts off two more groups of five, both as one, while he is talking. He is about to move to another person when he decides that four are enough. Holding the ten extra cards in his right hand, he presents the pack so that each person holding five can replace his group of cards. The magician remembers the order of the persons as they return their packets.

Noting the cards in his right hand, he throws them on the pack and gives the pack a riffle or a false cut. He calls upon the last person who returned the packet to name his chosen card. Given, the performer spells to it. The presence of the ten cards on top enables the magician to spell exactly to the mentally selected card, no matter which one of the five happened to be taken.

All dealt cards are immediately put back on the pack. The magician picks off the top five, fans them and reminds his audience that the selected card was chosen mentally from a group. He slides the five fanned cards to the bottom of the pack. He is now set to spell the card chosen by the third replacer, as he has ten indifferent cards upon that particular person's packet.

Repeating his previous maneuver, so as to replace ten cards, the magician spells the second replacer's card; and finally the first man's card.

This trick will be readily understood by experiment with the actual cards and the magician who uses it will find that it can be worked up to an excellent effect. It may be improved or varied by the use of a few false shuffles and great importance should be laid upon the fact that each chooser takes his card mentally from a group.

This trick is suitable for presentation with giant cards and should make a very fine showing on a small platform or stage. It is not essential to place the cards in the spectators' hands, although that facilitates matters when working with cards of ordinary size, at close range.

7. A SPELLING TRICK

This is an addition to a simple routine of spelling. The original arrangement is one used by Jack Gwynne, the well-known professional magician, who presents it as a short story with cards.

Tho performer offers to show just how the cards tell their own story. He takes a pack from his pocket and deals the cards faces down, one by one, spelling: "A-C-E--" turning up the third card to lay it aside. It is an ace. Continuing, he spells "T-W-O"—turning up a card and laying it aside on the letter "O." It is a two. He continues thus, turning up a three, a four, and so on. With "J-A-C-K--" he turns up a jack. With "Q-U-E-E-N--" and queen; and on the last letter—the "G" of "K-I-N-G"—he turns up a king, the final card of the pack!

Now for the addition. Thirteen cards are lying faces up, in order from ace up to king. The rest of the pack is back up, the cards together as they have been dealt one on the other. Picking up the face-up cards, the magician turns them face down and lays the packet on the other cards. He remarks that he has spelled values; he will now spell suits also.

"Take a king," he says. "The highest card—and hearts as a suit."

He deals the cards face down, spelling "K-I-N-G-O-F-H-E-A-R-T-S." He turns up the *next* card. It is the king of hearts.

"There are four suits," says the magician. "Four from king is nine. We have hearts; let's try diamonds—the nine of diamonds."

He spells the name of the card, dealing with it. He turns up the next card after the spelling. It is the nine of diamonds.

"Now for the blacks. Four from nine is five. We'll aim for the five of clubs."

The spelling follows. Right after the "S" the magician turns up the five of clubs.

"We have one more suit—spades. Four from five is one. Now for the ace of spades."

He spells down and when he finishes naming the ace of spades, letter by letter, the magician holds but one card. He turns it face up. It is the ace of spades.

To perform this trick, simply arrange the four aces on top of the deck; then four twos; four threes and so on. Note, however, the positions of four cards. The ace of spades should be the top ace of the aces. The five of clubs is the top of the fives; the nine of diamonds the top of the diamonds; the king of hearts on the very bottom of the pack.

The mere action of going through the deals as described, with their automatic card reversals, will make the trick work in the manner indicated.

8. AUTOMATIC SPELLING

The magician takes a number of cards from the pack. He gives the little packet to be shuffled. He asks a spectator to deal it into two heaps, one card at a time. The spectator is to look at the last card, remember it and lay it on either heap. The other heap is then dropped upon it.

We will suppose that the ace of hearts is the one selected. The magician takes the packet and asks for the name. It is given. He deals the top card of the packet face up, saying "A." The next card goes beneath the packet. Another is turned up, saying "C." Then one beneath. So on, spelling "E--O-F--H-E-A-R-T-S." When the magician announces the letter "S," he is holding a single card in his hand. He turns it up. It is the ace of hearts!

The secret depends upon the fact that when a group of eleven cards are spelled in this fashion, the sixth, or center card, will be the last one left. That is why the magician instructs the spectator to deal two heaps, look at the last card and lay it between the heaps, when they are gathered. It puts the chosen card right where he wants it.

All the cards in the packet must be spelled with exactly eleven letters. Here is a good line-up to use:

Ace of hearts, ace of spades, jack of clubs, six of spades, four of clubs, two of hearts, ten of spades, king of clubs, five of clubs, two of spades, ten of hearts.

There are just eleven cards in the group. Remember that those eleven are shuffled before one is selected. As a variation in the spelling, the magician may allow the person to spell mentally the name of his card, letter by letter, each time a card is dealt face up. The magician does not know the name of the card at all!

This is a trick that may call for repetition. Here is an interesting method that involves a different arrangement. The magician gives a cluster of cards to a spectator, tells him to shuffle the cards and to deal them into three heaps. Note—three heaps, instead of two. Then the person is told to look at the bottom card of any heap and to place the heap between the other two.

Once again, the magician gathers the packet and spells, turning up a card for each letter and putting one under after each letter. In this case he also arrives at the selected card for the grand finish.

In this method, twelve cards are utilized instead of eleven. They are all cards that may be spelled with twelve letters: for instance —five of hearts, queen of clubs, jack of spades, eight of clubs, seven of clubs, king of hearts, three of clubs, five of spades, jack of hearts, king of spades, four of spades, four of hearts.

With twelve cards, the eighth from the top will be the one left when the spelling deal is completed. By having the cards first dealt into three heaps, after the shuffle, there are three groups of four cards each.

The process of looking at the bottom card of any heap and placing that heap between the other two heaps automatically makes the chosen card lie number eight from the top. It is the most natural type of procedure. Yet all the magician needs to do is go through his spelling bee and he finishes with the desired card in his possession.

These two methods can be worked into a very effective combination. Take any pack and get eleven eleven-letter cards together; beneath them twelve twelve-letter cards. Deal off the eleven and emphasize the shuffle and choice of card after dealing two heaps. Spell to that card. Repeat the trick, letting the spectator spell silently. Shuffle the group back into the pack, or place it on the bottom and deal off twelve cards. Then use the three-heap method.

Never state the exact number of cards that you are using in the trick. Take them off casually and let the audience think that you are using a number at random. Persons attempting to duplicate the stunt will invariably get a mixture of cards that spell with varied numbers of letters.

This is one of the newest of all spelling tricks and one that affords real possibilities to the practical performer.

Chapter V

EASY CARD TRICKS

The tricks in this section can be performed anywhere at any time—with any pack of cards. They depend upon clever secrets or systems unknown to the spectators. None of them require any particular skill.

There are certain formulas in some of these tricks that will do the work, once the performer understands them. Each trick is a good one and an excellent program of card magic can be arranged from this section alone.

Practically every trick in this group is a mystery in itself, not depending upon any other method. Those persons already familiar with card magic will notice some novel ideas that may prove quite surprising to them. Certain principles have been adapted to new use and a close perusal of this section will prove of value to all card wizards.

1. CARD FOUND IN HAT

Someone shuffles the pack and gives you half, keeping the other portion. Drop your half of the pack in a hat and begin to shake it; put another hat over the top so the shaking can be done very violently and the cards will be sure to mix.

After demonstrating this, let the spectator take three cards from his half and insert them one by one, face downward, between the brims of the hats. As each card comes in, you shake the hats to mix it with those that are already in. The spectator, of course, knows each card he pushes in between the hats.

After lots of shaking, you remove the upper hat and reach into the lower, producing the chosen cards one by one—much to the astonishment of the chooser.

It's all done when you put your cards in the hat. Give them a good bend at the center. Best, shake them first, showing how they mix. Then gather them into a pack again and bend this time, the hat covering the movement.

The selected cards mix with the others, right enough, but they are straight while the others are curved and it is easy to distinguish them. Then, in gathering the remaining cards from the hat, bend them the other way to straighten them and no clue remains.

This trick mystified Blackstone when he first saw it performed —so the reader can be sure that it is a first class mystery when properly performed.

2. TWO NUMBER TRICK

A pack is shuffled. Any person takes it and notes a card a certain distance from the top—not more than ten or twelve cards down.

Taking the pack, the magician holds it behind his back and asks another person to name a number above twelve. The magician promises to put the chosen card at the new number—even though he does not know the chosen card nor its position!

He apparently does this, for when the cards are counted, the chosen card is at the new number.

There is a point to this trick that most persons fail to grasp. That is the method of counting. It begins not at one, but at the mentally selected number.

To make this clear, let us consider the trick just as handled by the performer. Suppose the fifth card is noted by the first party. Fifteen is the number named by the second person. Behind his back, the magician counts off fifteen cards, one by one, reversing their order. He drops them on top of the pack.

Giving the pack to the first spectator, he says: "Count to fifteen, starting the count with *your* number."

The person naturally counts: "five, six, seven," and so on until he says "fifteen." He will then be at the card he chose. This trick always works, no matter what the two numbers may be.

An interesting effect is to decide upon the higher number by using a pair of dice. Roll them often enough to get a total greater than twelve, adding the spots on each roll. Then proceed with the number thus determined.

3. BOTTOM TO TOP

This is a variation of the trick just described. It is given here as an alternate method. Many persons, seeing the two tricks, think that they are different in principle, whereas they are fundamentally the same.

Give the pack to a person. Tell him to pick any number less than ten and to remember the card that is that many from the bottom.

Take the pack and call for a number higher than ten. Suppose eighteen is given. Transfer eighteen cards from the bottom to the top, without changing their order. Move them in a group.

Now ask the first person's number. Suppose it is six. Counting from the top, begin with six. "Six, seven, eight—" a card for every number until you reach eighteen. That will be the card noted by the person as six from the bottom.

Let the man do the counting himself, if you wish, but always remember to have him start on his own number.

4. THOUGHT DISCOVERED

The magician spreads a pack so that about ten or twelve cards in the center are visible when the front of the pack is elevated toward the onlookers. A spectator is requested to note one of the visible cards mentally and to write its name on a sheet of paper.

The performer turns away while the name of the card is being written. The paper is folded and is given to another person. The magician shuffles the pack and gives it to the same person. The paper is then opened and the name of the mentally selected card is read. The person who has the pack looks through it for the chosen card. The card is missing—the magician immediately produces it from his pocket!

This is a very perplexing trick, yct it is not at all difficult. On the top of the pack the magician has ten or twelve cards that he has remembered—for instance: eight, queen, three, ten, two, seven, four, nine, king, ace.

This list, it will be noted, has no two cards of the same value—hence it is not necessary to remember suits. The magician may either arrange cards according to an order that he has previously memorized; or he can simply note the ten cards that happen to be on top of the pack, removing any that happen to be duplicated in value. Most persons will prefer to set up the cards to conform with their regular arrangement; then there can be no mistake.

At any rate, the magician cuts the pack by drawing some cards from the bottom and putting them on top. He keeps the two sections of the pack slightly separated and spreads the center cards —those which were originally on top. Thus the spectator must think of one of those cards.

The writing of the card gives the performer an excuse to turn away. He immediately lifts the cards that are above the known group and puts them back on the bottom; that is, he simply shifts the original bottom half of the pack back to where it belongs, so his ten known cards are again on top of the pack.

He then picks off at least ten cards and thrusts them in his pocket. Thus he has the ten known cards in his pocket—and one of those cards must be the one mentally selected.

When the slip of paper and the pack are handed to a spectator, the paper is naturally opened and read to learn the name of the missing card; while the spectator is looking for the card in the depleted pack, the magician simply puts his hand in his pocket and counts down to the required card. He, like the spectator, sees the name on the paper. Having his cards in a known order, he can easily find the right one. If the paper says "ten of spades," he counts eight, queen, three—*ten.*

He brings out the "missing" card and tosses it on the table, adding the additional cards to the pack at the first opportunity. The fact that the pack is depleted is never noticed.

5. TWENTY-FIVE CARDS

A great improvement over an older trick. A pack is shuffled. Five persons take five cards each. From his group, each person mentally selects a card. The magician gathers up the cards. He shows five cards and asks whose card is among them. A spectator says that he sees his card. The performer drops all cards but the chosen one. This is repeated until all five cards are discovered.

Here is the method. Let each person hold his group of five and remember one. He can shuffle his heap if he wishes. Go to the first person and ask for one card, face down. Then take a card from the second person, placing it on the card in your hand. Continue with persons three, four, five. Then go back to number one for another card.

You simply make the round, gathering cards one at a time until you have collected all twenty-five. But in this natural procedure, you have done something very important. You have arranged the cards in five groups: one, two, three, four, five—counting up from the bottom of the pack.

Now you take five cards from the top of those you hold. Fan them with the right hand. Although you alone know it, each of those cards has come from a different person. The card at the extreme left belongs to person one; the next to person two; three, four and five in order.

Show each person the fan. Ask if his card is there. If anyone says "yes," you immediately know which card it is, according to the person's number. Drop all cards but that one.

Now proceed with the next five cards—they will work just like the first five. Sometimes no one will have a card in the group. Just lay those cards aside. Sometimes two or three persons will see their card in the group. In that case drop one of the chosen cards, telling to whom it belongs; then drop the other and the third, if there is one.

Do all you can to make the trick effective. Do not even glance at the faces of the cards. That makes it so much the better. This trick, properly presented, will be a great mystery to those who witness it.

You are not limited to twenty-five cards. You can use thirty-six if you wish, involving six persons in the trick. You can also use forty-nine cards, with seven persons. Twenty-five is the best number for practical purposes as the trick goes more rapidly and is just as effective as when performed with a greater number of cards.

6. A DOUBLE PREDICTION

This is a very perplexing card trick. Read it carefully; then try it and you will be surprised to see how perfectly it works.

The magician takes twenty-one cards, among which is a conspicuous card—either the joker or the ace of spades. He writes two numbers—each on a separate slip of paper—without letting anyone see the numbers. He rolls up each piece of paper.

Someone removes the joker from the packet of cards and shuffles the cards. The performer spreads the cards. The joker is pushed into the heap. One person is told to remember the card just above the joker; the other person remembers the card just below.

Squaring the cards, the magician deals them into two heaps. He spreads each heap separately, asking the persons to note their cards but to say nothing whatever. He places the heaps together and again deals two heaps, each of which is shown, but no comment is asked.

The heaps are placed together; the cards are spread and someone removes the joker. The packet is now cut into two heaps, one of which is counted, to make sure that there are at least eight cards in it.

Now the papers are opened. One bears the number 6; the other the number 4. The chosen cards are named. One is discovered six from the top in one heap; the other is found four from the top in the other heap!

Let us explain. Read the directions carefully. After the two cards have been noted, one on each side of the inserted joker, the joker is left in the pack and two heaps are dealt, one card at a time, alternately, reversing the order of the cards. Both heaps are spread and shown in turn. In putting them together, be sure that the heap of eleven cards goes on top of the heap of ten.

Deal again—once more reversing the order of the cards—and show each heap. This time, again be sure to place the heap of eleven on top of the heap of ten.

Now fan the cards with the faces toward the audience and ask a person to remove the joker. Here is the important part. When the joker is removed, one chosen card will be exactly five cards above that spot; the other chosen card will be exactly five cards below.

Cut the pack at the place from which the joker is removed. You will have one card five from the top; the other card five from the bottom. Square up the pack and cut it into two portions, as near equal as possible. Count the cards in the bottom section, reversing their order as you do so. Result: one chosen card is five from the top in one heap; the other is five from the top in the other heap.

In this explanation, it is assumed that the two numbers written were 5 and 5—as that is the normal finish of the trick. But the reader will recall that in the description, we gave the numbers as 6 and 4. Certainly. They can be 6 and 4 just as well as 5 and 5. The crux lies in the cutting of the packet just after the removal of the joker. In cutting, draw one card from the top of the lower heap to the bottom of the upper, as you make the cut. Proceed just as with 5 and 5. But this time, the cards will turn up 6 and 4.

If you wish, you can make the cards come 7 and 3. This is done by drawing two cards from the top of the lower heap to the bottom of the upper as you make the cut. Now, if you prefer to have 8 and 2 as the final numbers, you can achieve that result by drawing three cards from the lower heap to the upper when you cut after the removal of the joker.

Of course you make up your mind what you are going to do before you start the trick. Then write the two numbers that you intend to use—each on a separate slip of paper. It is not wise to use 5 and 5, because the numbers are identical. 6 and 4 are better. But sometimes you may have to show the trick to people who have seen you do it before. So use 7 and 3 instead of 6 and 4.

Try this trick, using two conspicuous cards like red aces—one on each side of the joker. Go through the entire routine and you will then understand it. It is one of the best of all impromptu card tricks.

7. VANISHED CARD

Take a pack of cards and riffle the ends. Ask a person to think of any card that he sees. This is done. Again you riffle the pack.

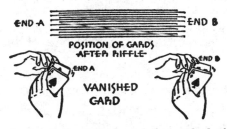

Note the projecting ends of cards and the method of riffling opposite ends of the pack.

To the person's amazement, the card is gone—even though you riffle the pack slowly, he cannot see it.

The Secret: Divide the pack beforehand and carefully dovetail shuffle the two heaps together so that they alternate. In pressing the two sections together, do not shove them all the way. One group projects at one end—the other group at the other end.

When you riffle one end of the pack, only the projecting cards will show. Thus the spectator can select only from that group. To make his card disappear, simply turn the pack around and riffle the other end. His card will not come into view.

To make the trick doubly effective, riffle end A before a spectator and let him select a card. Riffle end B before another spectator and let him think of a card. Then riffle end B for spectator A. His card has vanished. Riffle end A for spectator B. His card is gone.

Ask the names of the cards. Press the projecting ends together, turn the pack over and run through the cards face up. Both vanished cards have returned.

8. THE MYSTIC DISCOVERY

This is an unusual idea in card magic—a trick that is very puzzling, yet which offers no great difficulties in presentation. It is a trick that must be thoroughly understood and which should be practiced to give it the neat precision which it requires. For the trick is most effective when done in an easy, efficient style.

The magician takes any pack after it has been shuffled. He holds it in his left hand and riffles the cards with his right, doing this slowly so that the spectators can see the faces of the cards as they fall.

"Think of any card that you see," says the magician. "If you note two or three, settle your mind upon one. You have it? Very well, I shall deal Bridge hands."

He then proceeds to deal the pack into four piles of thirteen each, which he designates as South, West, North and East. Picking up a hand, he spreads it and studies the cards for a moment. He turns the faces toward the person who chose the card.

"Is your card in this hand?" he asks.

If the reply is affirmative, the magician uses that heap; if negative, he shows the next hand—and so on, until he learns which pack contains the mentally selected card.

"That makes my chances a little better," says the magician. "I'm pretty sure I have your card. Our thoughts are working well."

He lays the heap face down upon the table and asks the spectator to name his card. The card is named. The magician calmly turns up the top card of the pile and reveals the card that was mentally selected.

Now for the explanation. In riffling the cards, the magician begins while he is telling what he wants done. He does not turn the faces so they can be seen until he has run through about twenty cards rather rapidly—roughly, he has just about reached the center of the pack before the spectator has a real opportunity to glimpse the face of a card.

As the magician urges the person to think of a card, he lets the cards riffle slowly, one by one, allowing plenty of opportunity for the person to take any one of the cards that he sees. Approximately twelve cards are allowed to fall in this fashion; then, assuming that a card has been taken, the magician lets the rest of the cards riffle rapidly.

In brief, the wizard, despite the opportunity he seems to have given has actually limited the choice to one of a dozen cards, all located more than twenty from the bottom. When the heaps are dealt, there will be thirteen in each. They are dealt carefully; thus the bottom cards of the pack fall on top of the heaps.

Considering each heap individually, we can eliminate the top five cards and the bottom four. The selected card is sure to be either 6, 7, 8 and 9 from the top of its particular group. This is allowing sixteen cards—plenty of margin. But the magician wants an even better percentage. When he picks up one of the hands and spreads it, he is careful to keep the sixth and seventh cards out of sight behind the eighth. He allows a brief glance at the fan and asks if the spectator sees his card.

If the spectator sees his card in one of the heaps, the wizard knows that the card is either number eight or number nine from the top of the heap. Should the spectator fail to see his card in any hand, the explanation is obvious—to the magician only. He knows that the chosen card must be six or seven in its particular heap. So he chides the spectator for not looking closely enough and goes through the hands again. This time he spreads all of the cards—so the spectator naturally sees the chosen one. Thus the magician learns its heap.

Now for the finish. By the elimination process just described, the magician limits the chosen card to one of two—either six or seven in a certain heap; or eight or nine in that heap. He switches the cards around a bit and in the action puts one of the possible cards on top of the heap; the other on the bottom. In a positive manner he lays the heap face down and calls for the name of the card. When it is given, the magician either turns up the top card or turns over the entire heap to show the bottom card—according to which one is named. Either revelation is surprising to the audience. Knowing the proper card, the magician simply uses the correct discovery.

9. THE SAME NUMBER

A very neat card trick. Offer a pack to a person and ask him to shuffle it. Then tell him to count off any number of cards, while you are watching—at least ten cards—and to give you the remainder.

The person counts, say, sixteen. When you receive the balance of the pack, you ask him to lift his sixteen cards and drop them on. You hold the pack squared and show that all cards are even. Then, to demonstrate ease in counting, you lift off a bunch of cards and throw them on the table, announcing that you have taken sixteen. Counted, the statement proves correct.

It's all done when you receive the pack. Take the cards in the left hand, with the thumb across the back of the pack. Catch the ends of the pack with the right hand—thumb at one end and fingers at the other. Bend the ends up.

When the sixteen cards are put on the pack, square it and hold the cards tightly pressed. There is a space between the sixteen cards and the rest of the pack, but by pressing with the left thumb, you hide this fact.

Release pressure and the straight sixteen cards will raise, leaving the break below them. Simply lift off all cards above the break and throw them on the table. You have taken off the sixteen.

Shuffling the pack in dovetail fashion will destroy all traces of bent-up cards.

10. THE TWENTY CARD TRICK

For years magicians have been performing a trick with twenty cards that is highly effective and will always remain so. Twenty cards are dealt in piles of two cards each. Different persons are allowed to look at pairs and memorize them.

The magician gathers the pairs, and deals the cards haphazard in four rows of five cards each, faces up. He points out the four horizontal rows and asks a spectator to indicate the row or rows in which his cards appear. As soon as this is done, the magician picks up the two chosen cards. This is repeated with the other selections.

The secret of this trick lies in the fact that the apparent haphazard dealing is actually in accordance with a system. The magician puts each card in a particular place for it. Now the time-honored system for this trick depended upon the use of four Latin words—mutus, nomen, dedit, cocis—and for years no one thought of departing from it. Somehow it seemed as though only Latin words would do—and the worst of it was that the word "cocis" is not Latin at all.

An English formula is more preferable. It is more easy to remember; it has some meaning; and it will confuse those who know the old trick and who think that the antiquated system is the only one that can possibly work. Several English formulas have been devised for this trick, and now we present one that is entirely new. Note the four words in this table:

RIDER
HOODS
CINCH
TENTS

There are ten letters used in the four words and each letter appears twice. Every combination of letters is different. For instance, O appears twice in row 2; N appears in rows 3 and 4; E appears in rows 1 and 4—and so on. Observe these combinations.

Now in dealing out the twenty cards to make four rows of five each, the performer visualizes his code as though it were inscribed in large letters upon the table. He puts the first card face up at the spot where he pictures the first R; the second card is set where the second R should be. Next he places a card for I; another card for I; then proceeds with D and D—and continues thus.

When a spectator indicates that his chosen cards are in rows 2 and 3, the magician simply repeats his formula mentally and he finds that the letter H appears in both "hoods" and "cinch"; therefore the two cards are on the spots where the letter H should be.

So much for the bare outline of this very effective trick. Let us consider presentation. To do the trick properly, the magician should allow the pack to be shuffled; then deal his ten piles of two —*faces down*. While the magician's back is turned, spectators are allowed to look at pairs. All the pairs are then gathered in haphazard form. The magician has not seen the face of a single card.

He makes his deal in careless fashion, creating the idea that he is endeavoring to mix things even more. Then, when he begins to pick out the chosen cards as the rows are mentioned to him, he will be rewarded by a perplexed group of spectators and he will realize just how effective this twenty card trick can be.

11. IMPROVED TWENTY CARDS

Not content with giving the reader an entirely new formula for the twenty cards, we shall now explain a method of distribution which requires no words whatever. In this system, the trick appears the same to the onlookers. But the magician can begin his deal anywhere, with no danger of forgetting or becoming mixed with imaginary words.

This new system depends simply upon a numerical arrangement which will be entirely clear at the first reading. It enables the magician to deal the cards in a most careless fashion.

Picture the four rows of five cards each, considered thus:

$$1 - 2 - 3 - 4 - 1$$
$$1 - 2 - 3 - 4 - 2$$
$$1 - 2 - 3 - 4 - 3$$
$$1 - 2 - 3 - 4 - 4$$

The cards in each row are simply numbered 1 to 4 from left to right. The last card in each row is the key card, giving the number of the row—hence here the numbers run 1, 2, 3, 4 from top to bottom.

This is the simple chart which the performer visualizes on the table in place of the cabalistic words. He gathers his twenty cards and begins to place them on the table, starting at any point. Suppose he sets down the middle card of row 2. That is card 3 in row 2. Very well: the next card is placed as card 2 in row 3. When the magician places a card at position 2 in row 1, he simply follows with a card at position 1 in row 2.

The purpose of the key cards or positions at the right should now be apparent. In each row, its own number appears twice. Thus when the magician puts a card at position 2 in row 2, he follows by putting a card at the right end of row 2—where the duplicate number 2 is present.

Let us suppose that twenty cards have been dealt by this formula. Using different letters to indicate each pair of cards, we will have a layout in this fashion:

        D B C G D
        B J A H J
        C A E F E
        G H F I I

The pointing out of the cards is a matter of extreme simplicity with this system. A spectator mentions that his cards appear in rows 2 and 3. The magician simply picks up the third card in the second row and the second card in the third row. If both cards are in row 3, pick up the third card and the key (fifth) card. If cards are in rows 1 and 4, the fourth card of the first and the first card of the fourth are the ones the magician wants.

12. MATHEMATICAL DISCOVERY

This is an idea used by Paul Noffke, the clever card wizard. Its purpose is to enable the performer to tell the name of a card which he does not know.

A spectator has chosen a card. Tell him to remember its numerical value (ace, one; jack, eleven; queen, twelve; king, thirteen)—also the suit of the card.

Tell him to double the value of the card.

Then tell him to add three to the total.

Tell him to multiply the complete total by five.

This done, ask him to concentrate on the suit.

If the card is a diamond, he must add one.

If it is a club, he must add two.

If it is a heart, he must add three.

If it is a spade, he must add four.

He must then tell you the final total.

From it, you immediately divine the name of the selected card.

The secret is to subtract fifteen from the final total. You will have a number of two figures—possibly three. The last figure gives you the suit (diamonds 1, clubs 2, hearts 3, spades 4) while the first figure or figures give you the value.

Examples: Jack of clubs.

11 doubled is 22. Add 3—25. Multiply by 5—125. Add 2 (for clubs) making 127. You are told that number.

Subtract 15 mentally. Result, 112. Last figure (2) means clubs. First figures (11) mean jack.

With the five of hearts.

5 doubled is 10. Add 3—13. Multiply by 5—65. Add 3 (for hearts) making 68. You are told that number.

Subtract 15 mentally. Result, 53. Last figure (3) means hearts. First figure (5) means five spot.

This is a very effective routine and it is particularly valuable when a troublesome spectator takes a card and makes it impossible for you to go ahead with the trick as you have intended it.

Remember that the spectator performs all his calculation without telling you a word about the card itself. He can do it mentally or on paper. All you ask is the total. The total does not appear to give you any clue to the card, because no one knows your secret system of deducting 15.

13. THREE HEAPS

A spectator deals three cards faces up. He counts the value of one card and turns it down. He adds enough cards to it to make fifteen. For example, if the card is a seven, he deals eight cards on it.

He repeats this process with the other two cards. Then the magician comes in and takes the cards that remain. He quickly tells the total value of the three cards on the bottoms.

The system is this: Count the cards that remain. Disregard four of them. The rest will be the same as the total of the hidden cards.

Face cards are usually counted as ten in this trick. If desired, jack can be eleven; queen, twelve; king, thirteen. It makes no difference.

Typical layout of three heaps, with additional cards added to make totals of fifteen.

While the trick is very bewildering to those who do not understand it, it is readily understood if we consider it with three aces as the bottom cards. That means fifteen cards in each heap. The total is forty-five. That leaves seven cards over. The total of the aces is three. So four cards must be disregarded.

Now, if a two spot is put in place of one of the aces, the total of the bottom cards becomes five instead of four. But the use of a two spot means one less card in that heap—one card more in the surplus. Hence the rule works, no matter what the value of the base cards may be.

14. MANY HEAPS

This effect is similar to the three heap trick; but in this instance the face cards must count as ten and after a card is placed on the table, other cards are added to make the total twelve.

For instance, a seven is laid face down. That means five cards must be dealt on it. If a king is laid face down, two cards must be added.

There is no set limit to the number of heaps. The dealer may use three as in the other trick; but he may use more—five, six, or seven—in fact, he may continue until he has no more cards to make up totals.

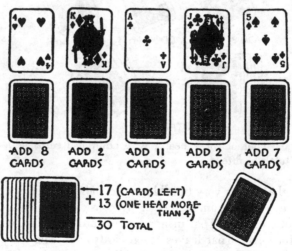

Typical layout of five heaps, indicating additional cards making totals of twelve.

The performer recommends that at least five heaps be used—if possible. When he returns, he takes the extra cards, looks at the heaps, and names the total of the bottom cards.

To understand this, let us consider it with four heaps. Four aces on the bottoms mean forty-eight cards used. There will be four cards left over. That is the total. In other words, with four heaps in use, the extra cards tell the total exactly.

Now when the performer returns, he counts the extra cards and disregards four of the heaps. For each additional heap, he simply adds thirteen. Why? Because if we had four kings as bottom cards, with two cards on each, there would be a total of forty extra cards. Now the formation of a fifth heap with an ace on the bottom would require twelve of those forty cards. It would also add one to the total of the under cards. That means thirteen.

Thus if we have six heaps and twelve cards left over the total of the under cards will be 13 plus 13 plus 6—32. With seven heaps and nine cards over, the total will be 13 plus 13 plus 13 plus 9—48.

If a spectator decides to use only three heaps, simply subtract thirteen from the total number of cards left over. If he uses only two heaps, subtract twenty-six from the remaining cards.

Four heaps is the basis of the formula and there is no difficulty whatever in determining the totals. The trick is a good one to repeat, because the spectators will try varied numbers of heaps and will find this experiment more perplexing as it continues.

15. NAME IN ENVELOPE

The performer lays a pack of cards on the table. He asks someone to cut the pack. Picking up a sealed envelope, the magician lays it on one heap. The cut is completed. The card below the envelope is noted. The envelope is torn open. Inside is found a slip of paper bearing the name of the card.

There are two ways of doing this trick. First, by using the method described under the title "An Easy Force." The magician knows the top card of the pack and lays the envelope upon it when the cut is made, having someone put the rest of the cards on the envelope.

The other method can be used with a shuffled pack—in which the magician cannot possibly know the location of any card. He has previously removed the desired card from the pack and it is lying beneath the envelope, projecting over the edge of the table.

The magician picks up the card with the envelope. In placing the envelope on one heap of cards he simply adds the hidden card to the heap. Since that card corresponds with the name written on the paper in the envelope, the trick is sure to work.

Chapter VI

ADVANCED CARD TRICKS

Tricks partially dependent upon sleights form the contents of this section. In certain cases, optional methods are given so that skill is eliminated. In most of the tricks, a very small element of skill is all that is required.

The reader will find various references to the sleights listed in Chapter One. Most of the problems in the following pages are complete tricks in themselves. The "Card in the Pocket" is one— and we present five methods of performing this ever-popular trick. We feel sure that the adaptations utilized in it will be of special interest to the reader.

Effort has been made to reduce skill to the minimum. These tricks are within the range of any reader who tries them. Some performers will choose to show them with all the elaborations possible, thus adding to the effect. That is purely a matter of individual choice.

1. CARD IN THE POCKET

The effect of this trick is that the spectator takes the pack and counts down any number of cards, noting the name of any card and its number from the top of the pack.

The magician returns and receives the pack. Glancing through it, he removes and pockets a card. He asks the spectator's number —not the card. The number being given, the magician counts down that far. The spectator's card is not there, so the magician obligingly removes it from his pocket.

There are several methods of performing this trick. They are given herewith, so that the performer can vary them and thus repeat the trick effectively.

First Method: The performer takes a card from near the bottom of the pack and pockets it. He palms it in his pocket and adds it to the pack when he brings his hand from the pocket.

When the location of the card is given, the wizard counts to it and naturally he stops one short, due to the secretly added card. Suppose the chosen card to be ninth from the top. When he reaches nine, the performer deals the card face down on the table, with the others. It is really the eighth card. Looking at it, the spectator finds that it is not his card.

Meanwhile the performer, just as attention is on the card on the table, palms the real ninth card. Going to his pocket he brings it forth—apparently the card that he put there beforehand.

Second Method: In this variation of the trick, the performer puts the top card in his pocket and leaves it there. Suppose the number is nine. He counts off nine cards with his right hand, each card on the one before, so that their order is reversed. He pushes the next card (really the tenth) from the pack and replaces the right hand cards on the pack.

The spectators look at the card on the table and see that it is not the chosen one. Meanwhile the performer palms the card now on top of the pack, reaches in his pocket and brings it out showing it to be the chosen card. He leaves the odd card in his pocket, later replacing it in the pack.

Third Method: In this version, the performer secretly notes the top card of the pack.* He tells the spectator to deal off any number, one by one; to look at the next card and put the dealt cards on top.

For instance, the spectator deals off eight, looks at the ninth and puts the eighth back on again. The magician returns and looks through the pack for the top card. It is now at number eight, due

* By means of the "glimpse"—third method.

to the reversal. He takes the card below it (the ninth) and pockets it.

He asks the number. He is told nine. He deals off nine and shows the last one. Not the chosen card. Out it comes from the pocket. This method eliminates the palming.

Fourth Method: Here the performer gives a spectator a slip of paper and tells him to write down any three figures—all different —forming a number. He is then to reverse the number and subtract the smaller from the larger.

This being done, add the figures in the result and look at the card that number from the top of the pack. The pack is first shuffled by the spectator.

The secret is the fact that the result will always be 18.

Examples:

	451	603	812	594
	−154	−306	−218	−495
	297	297	594	99

In each case the figures of the result (297, 594, 99) total 18. Knowing this, the magician simply runs down to the eighteenth card and puts it in his pocket, performing the rest of the trick in the accustomed fashion of asking for the number, counting down to it and showing that the chosen card is gone.

Fifth Method: In this version, the magician introduces a pair of dice. He tells someone to roll them and note the total; to pick up one of the dice, add the bottom side and roll it again, adding the new number that turns up. The dice are left on the table. The total is remembered and the card at that number in the pack is the one noted.

The magician, on returning, rolls the dice a few times as though that had some important value. He looks through the pack and puts a card in his pocket. On counting down, the chosen card is missing. It is the one he took.

Simply add seven to the dice as they lie. Thus three and two are rolled—five. The two is turned over; its under side is a five— adding makes ten. The die is rolled again and turns up four. Total, fourteen. The fourteenth card is noted.

When the magician views the dice, he notes four and three. He adds seven to that total, arriving at fourteen. This gives him the position of the card—fourteenth.

The trick with the dice depends on the fact that opposite sides of a single die always total seven. Yet even people who know it will be fooled by the peculiar way in which the dice are rolled.

Summary: By employing the various methods of performing the card in the pocket, the magician can repeat the trick a number of times or exhibit it differently each time he is requested to perform it.

2. FOUR ACE CHANGE

This is where the laugh is turned on the audience. The magician holds the pack between his hands and shows the ace of clubs on the bottom. He deals the ace face downward. He then puts the next card on top of the pack.

He shows the ace of hearts, the ace of diamonds and the ace of spades, dealing each one and putting the alternate cards on top.

But by this time the spectators know that he is bluffing. For the magician has been showing three spots instead of aces, covering the end spots with his fingers. He has not only done it crudely; he has given it away with the ace of spades. For instead of appearing with a large, ornamental ace, that ace has been shown as only a small spot.

When the magician states that he will transform the aces into threes, everyone demands to see the aces. So the magician obligingly turns them faces up and shows that they are actually aces after all.

That turns the laugh. When the magician decides to go on with the trick, he pushes the cards around a bit, turns them faces up and shows that they are now threes.

Here is the method. The bottom card is really a three; then comes an ace, a three, an ace, a three, an ace, a three (spades) and an ace.

Showing the first three with the fingers covering the end spots, the magician announces that he will deal it on the table. Actually, he uses the "glide"* drawing back the card and dealing an ace in its stead. He transfers the three spot to the top of the pack without showing its face.

He continues thus, showing each three in turn, but really dealing aces. So at last, he has four aces on the table while the threes have been transferred to the top of the pack, each in its proper turn.

The magician then turns up the aces after a long protest has been registered by the audience. At this point he acts as though the trick is ended, with the joke being turned on the spectators.

But he really takes advantage of the situation to exchange the aces for the threes. This is done by the "bottom change"—a sleight fully described in Blackstone's "Secrets of Magic." It is given briefly here, as in this case the sleight can be done very slowly, for the audience does not know that anything else is coming.

The left thumb, on top of the pack, has pushed the four top cards well to the left. The right hand picks up the aces and holds them faces down, between the first and second fingers. The right hand approaches the left. The lower fingers of the left hand open to receive the aces. The right hand removes the threes between the thumb and forefinger. These cards are immediately dropped on the table.

The magician can then show the cards as threes when he wishes. There is an interesting bit of by-play, however, that adds to the effect of the trick. Moving the cards around, the magician peeks at the faces and selects the three of diamonds. He uses it as an indicator to point at the others—without revealing the face of the card.

"It's a funny thing," he remarks. "You thought these aces were other cards, didn't you? What's that? You thought they were the threes! Take this ace of diamonds, for instance. Look at it—you thought it was a three—"

So saying, he skims the ace upward in the air, by holding it between his two first fingers, and twirling it edgewise. As the spec-

* A sleight explained elsewhere in this book.

tators look upward at the spinning card, it actually appears to be an ace, for the end spots merge with the center one.

When the card strikes the floor, it proves to be a three spot after all. The magician then invites an inspection of the other three cards that are on the table. They, like the diamond, are threes instead of aces.

The success of this trick depends largely upon showmanship and the performer who practices it to gain effect will find that it is a most excellent deception.

3 · THREE CARD MONTE

This is a very clever version of the three card monte trick, which can be acquired with little practice and is quite deceptive.

The magician holds three cards in a fan—faces toward the au-

THREE CARD MONTE

How the center ace is shifted secretly to the right. The right thumb performs the action.

dience. One card is behind the other two—that is the center card of the fan, which we will assume to be the ace of spades.

The magician calls attention to the position of the ace of spades, which is flanked by the ace of hearts and the ace of clubs. He turns the cards face downward and asks someone to remove the ace of spades. Naturally, the person takes the center card. Imagine his surprise when he discovers that he is holding the ace of hearts instead of the ace of spades!

There is a little sleight used in this trick. Note the position of the cards. The ace of hearts is the front one; the ace of clubs next; the ace of spades behind the other two, peering from between them.

When the cards are turned face down, the right thumb, which is behind the three cards, moves to the right, swinging the ace of spades to the right position. The center card is now the ace of hearts. A person naturally takes it as the ace of spades. The swing of the arm completely covers the sliding of the ace of spades to the right and the spectator has no idea that a change has been made.

4. THE TRAVELING ACE

This follows the "three card monte" that was just explained. It is an old trick, utilized to a new purpose. The reader will recall that the three cards used in the "monte" were the aces of clubs, spades and hearts. There was a reason.

After demonstrating that the ace of hearts mysteriously takes the place of the ace of spades, the performer kindly consents to do the trick again. He turns his back for a moment, while he arranges the cards. He says that he will use the ace of diamonds. Actually, he has the ace of diamonds in his pocket. He uses the ace of hearts to appear as the ace of diamonds.

This time, the red ace is the back card. In setting it behind the angle formed by the other two aces, the wizard fixes matters so that only the point of the heart is visible—thus the card appears as the ace of diamonds.

The reader will remember that in the "monte" trick, the spectators got the ace of hearts instead of the ace of spades. The performer, now showing the three cards, tells them he will make it easy for them to get the ace of diamonds—for it is in the center.

Showing the fanned cards, he turns them face down, making his slide and letting a spectator get the center card—one of the black aces.

"You didn't get the ace of diamonds?" comes the magician's question, as he drops the other two cards faces down on the table. "I'll tell you why. It's here!"

And he draws the missing ace of diamonds from his pocket!

5. THE HOAX WITH ACES

This is an old trick, but it is always a good one. It is performed with two aces—the red ones—and a confederate helps the magician.

The pack is divided into two packets. Upon one heap, the magician places the ace of hearts. He shows the ace of diamonds and puts it on the other heap. Lifting this heap he puts it on the ace of hearts, but as he does so, he quickly pulls the ace of diamonds from the top and drops it on the ace of hearts ahead of the descending packet.

The magician blandly states that the two aces will be found together. He deals cards from the bottom of the pack, turning them face up, one by one. At last he comes to the first red ace. He states that the next card he draws off will be the other ace. Sure enough, it is.

Everyone laughs at the crudity of this trick and the confederate, with a wink at the audience, asks the magician to "do it again." The magician consents. But while he is showing the ace of diamonds to everyone, the confederate slyly takes a few cards from the upper heap and drops them on the ace of hearts.

Now, when the magician goes through his crude feat of slipping the ace of diamonds on to the lower heap, the laugh appears to be on him—for the aces will not be together.

The magician proceeds unwittingly, declaring that the two red aces will come together as he deals cards from the bottom. A red ace comes into view and the magician is emphatic that the next card will be the other ace. Everyone else laughs. So the magician brings forth the card and it actually is the missing ace!

Here is the method: The magician knows the card directly under the ace of hearts—say, the five of clubs. He knows what the confederate has done—that the aces will really be apart. But he deals away, pulling each card from the bottom and turning it face up until he sees the five of clubs. That tells him that the ace of hearts is next.

He does not deal the ace of hearts. Instead, he draws it back by means of the "glide"* and continues dealing other cards. The ace of diamonds comes up. To bring the ace of hearts next, the magician simply draws it forth, for it is on the bottom, waiting for him.

6. THE ACE HOAX

(*With Improvements*)

The effect of this trick is similar to the "Hoax with Aces." The magician shows how he can make the red aces come together even though placed apart—but the crudity of his method fools no one.

Offering to do the trick again, he places the ace of hearts on one heap and shows the ace of diamonds. The confederate quickly seizes the ace of hearts and pockets it. The magician does not see the action.

The magician puts the ace of diamonds on top of the pack and makes the crude transfer, slipping it to the lower heap. When he says that the cards will come together—two red aces—no one believes him. But the magician has the last laugh, for the red aces come together and the confederate expresses surprise at finding a different card in his pocket.

In this case, the deception begins with the exhibition of the ace of hearts, before it is placed upon the lower half of the pack. The magician picks up the ace of hearts with another card on top of it. He shows these two cards as one; by bending the cards slightly outward, they hold firmly together and appear as one card.

Thus two cards go on the lower heap. While the magician is showing the ace of diamonds, the confederate quickly steals the top card of the lower heap. He does not have time to show its face. Everyone takes for granted that it is the ace of hearts. But the ace of hearts still remains on the lower heap.

So when the magician employs his crude maneuver, he actually brings the two aces together and he can deal the cards one by one from the bottom, arriving at the united aces.

In doing the trick in this form, the deal from the bottom is not

* Described in Chapter One.

essential. All through the trick, the magician can simply spread the pack face up and show the two aces side by side.

7. TRAVELING CARD TRICK

The magician uses two envelopes and a pack of cards. He asks a spectator to count off twelve cards. The spectator does this. The magician then counts off twelve cards.

He verifies the spectator's count, counting the twelve cards again. He puts these twelve cards in one envelope. He seals the envelope. A spectator holds it.

The magician verifies the count of his own twelve cards. He puts his twelve in the other envelope. A spectator holds it—the envelope being sealed.

"Pass!" Three cards go from one envelope to the other. Nine in one envelope, fifteen in the other. Spectators open the envelopes themselves and do the counting!

Here's the method: Between the two envelopes the performer puts three cards, faces down. The envelopes are face to face. They are shown casually together. No one realizes that three cards are hidden between them.

A spectator counts off twelve cards and places them on the table. The performer counts off twelve—apparently—but actually he uses the "false count"* and only counts off nine, making them appear as twelve.

When he verifies the spectator's count, he counts the cards upon the envelopes. He picks up the envelopes and lets the cards slide into his right hand. Needless to state, the hidden cards go with them. One envelope is dropped; the fifteen cards are sealed in the other.

The magician quickly verifies the count of his own cards, but he uses the elusive "false count" once more—so the packet which presumably contains twelve actually consists of nine cards. These are placed in the second envelope which is sealed. The rest is merely a matter of showmanship.

* Explained in the first chapter of this book.

This trick is not at all difficult, but it should be presented convincingly. Afterward, spectators will believe that they did all the counting themselves. Great importance should be attached to the fact that the sealed envelopes are held by the spectators.

Also, the magician should see to it that the envelopes look the same. He can ask for the spectators to select one. The magician then offers to make cards pass from it or into it—as the case may be. This should be done in a casual manner.

He can also ask for a number of cards—say between one and four—the response usually being "three." This makes it look as though the spectators decided upon the number that was to be used in the passing.

Should "two" be stated—the only other choice—the magician gets out of it by turning to another person and saying—"I wanted you to decide the number—but since two has been mentioned, we can use two—and one for you, which makes three altogether."

8. IMPROVED POCKET TO POCKET

Have a person cut a pack of cards. Let him count the cards in his heap. Suppose there are twenty-four. That leaves twenty-eight with you, as you verify by counting. For there are fifty-two cards in a pack.

Give the person your heap and let him put it in his inside pocket. Take his heap and put it in your inside pocket. Presto! Three cards leave his pocket and come into yours. He finds that his stock of twenty-eight is reduced to twenty-five, while you now have twenty-seven instead of twenty-four.

Anyone can count the cards when they are brought from the pockets. Absolutely no deception, so it seems. Especially as a borrowed pack is used.

This is the way. Before starting the trick, smuggle three cards from the pack and put them in your pocket. Let a person take part of the pack, count it, and give it to you—twenty-four cards for example. Meanwhile you count yours as three more than are really there, using the "false count." This is not absolutely necessary as you deduct from fifty-two, but it adds to the effect and as you are merely counting as a matter of routine, no one watches you closely.

Your cards really go into his pocket—three short. His go into your pocket and there they join the three cards that are awaiting them. The trick is as good as done.

9. A FOUR ACE TRICK

This is an effective version of the four ace trick, aided by the use of four special envelopes. The magician exhibits the four aces. He deals them in a row on the table. He adds three cards to each ace. He puts each group in an envelope—each envelope having an open front, so the center of the ace is visible.

At the magician's command, all the aces gather in one envelope, leaving four indifferent cards in each of the other envelopes.

The Method: When the four aces are first shown, they are held in a fan. Behind the last ace are three cards, bunched together. When the aces are laid on the pack and redealt in a row, only one of the cards is really an ace. Note that the uppermost of the real aces should be the ace of spades. The hidden cards are the five of diamonds, five of clubs, and three of hearts.

Another system of adding the three indifferent cards is to have them lying face up beneath the envelopes. The magician starts to remove the envelopes and lays down the fan of aces at the same time, covering the three extra cards. Then the cards are closed and dropped faces down on the pack.

With a row of four cards—apparently aces—but only the ace of spades on the table, the magician deals the three genuine aces on the ace of spades. Then three indifferent cards are placed on each of the supposed aces—twelve cards in all. The packets are now inserted in the envelopes. The open-cut sides of the envelopes are underneath. So when the packets are in the envelopes, the magician can turn over the envelopes and apparently show an ace in each one. The center spots of the fives and the three look like the single spots of the aces.

The envelopes are inverted again and laid in a square—one envelope at each corner. The magician calls for a number: "one, two, three or four." Whatever is given, he counts around the square to the ace of spades. He can start his count wherever he wants, so it does not matter what number is given!

After "selecting" the ace of spades in this fashion, the magician gives that envelope into the keeping of a spectator. Removing the cards from one envelope, he shuffles them, spreads them and shows that the ace is missing. He does the same with each of the other envelopes. At the finish, all four aces are discovered in the envelope which is held by the spectator.

This routine can be performed without the envelopes, but it is not nearly so convincing. The use of the special envelopes, which are easily made, adds much to the trick. The envelopes should be slightly larger than a playing card. Envelopes that open at the end are the best.

Chapter VII

SPECIAL CARD TRICKS

In this section we have placed tricks which require a certain setup or arrangement of cards. With a bit of preparation, it is possible to produce effects in card magic which cannot be accomplished in a totally impromptu exhibition.

We have not, however, included tricks that need fake cards or special appliances. This section introduces a number of interesting ideas in card magic and will be of great value to the reader who is in search of novelty.

Some of the tricks require so little preparation that they can be introduced almost anywhere and will be of use to the impromptu magician as well as to the performer who has his own cards all ready in his pocket.

1. THE TEN CARD CIRCLE

This trick is simple but puzzling. It is described here in detail for two reasons: first, because it is a good impromptu trick in this form; second, because the trick which follows is a great improvement that will be more readily understood when one knows the circle method.

The cards, numbered from ace to ten, are arranged faces up like the circle of a clock dial. A spectator is invited to *think* of one card. Another person is asked to *point out* one card. Suppose, for instance, that the eight is thought of and the five is pointed out.

Noting the five, the magician adds ten, and says: "I want you—" the spectator who is thinking of the card—"to count from the five spot. Begin the count with your own number and count to fifteen, moving to the left."

The spectator does this. He places his finger on the five and says "eight"; he touches the four and says "nine"; he continues in this manner and when he reaches fifteen—the number set by the magician—he is astonished to find that his count has ended on the very card he chose—the eight spot!

This trick always works. Simply follow the system as described and the result will be the same. Remember to add ten to the number indicated.

To make the trick more perplexing, it is wise to use cards of different suits, but in numerical order, and to lay them faces down. Let a person peek at one card while your back is turned. Another person points out a card at random and turns it face up. Add ten to its value, tell the thinker to start his count at that card, and to begin with his own number. The fact that he arrives on his own card which is face down makes the experiment doubly perplexing.

2. IMPROVED CARD CIRCLE

The greatest improvement in this trick—which makes it a new effect—is the fact that the card circle is used in theory but not in practice. To the spectators, it appears to be a dealing trick.

A pack is shuffled. Ten cards are dealt off by a spectator. He notes the position of any card from the bottom of the heap—say six of clubs, four from the bottom.

The magician takes the heap. He asks someone to name a number below ten. Take eight for instance. The magician calmly removes eight cards from the bottom of the packet, saying: "Eight and ten make eighteen—we will count to eighteen beginning with your number—" pointing to the person who is thinking of the fourth card from the bottom.

The person says his number is four. The magician deals a card, counting "four." He does not drop the card to the table—he puts it under the heap from which he is dealing. He repeats this with the next cards, counting "five, six" and so on—thus he has an inexhaustible heap from which to deal. When he reaches eighteen, the number which he designated, the spectator's thought-of card is the one that he turns up. If he wishes, the performer can let the spectator do the dealing in the fashion described, counting to himself and ending on the mentally selected card. That is a good method to use as a repeat.

Keep these points in mind: the card mentally selected is noted counting from the *bottom* of the packet. The number of cards named by the second spectator are shifted in a group from *bottom to top*. The deal is made from the top, with the cards faces down, the cards going to the bottom one by one. The final card is turned up.

3. A MYSTIC PREDICTION

In this trick, the magician volunteers to make a remarkable prediction. He writes something upon a sheet of paper and folds it. He removes a pack of cards from its case and puts the folded paper therein. He arranges some cards in five heaps which lie in a row upon the table. He remarks that these heaps may be counted singly, from left to right.

A person is requested to select a heap, the magician making it plain that the heap selected will be the one used. "Take any heap," are his words, "and you will discover that I have foretold the very heap which you chance to choose!"

A heap is designated. The paper is taken from the card case. It is opened. It bears the words: "You will choose the five heap." This prediction is verified. The magician proves unmistakably that the chooser has taken the "five" heap.

The important secret of this experiment is that any one of the heaps will fill the bill. Each can be made to pass as the so-called "five" heap. This depends upon the arrangement of the cards.

One heap consists of all the five spots. Should it be chosen, the magician turns it face upward and shows that it has four fives. He shows the faces of the other cards. There are no fives among them.

If this heap is taken, the magician says: "This, you see, is the 'five' heap—all five spots."

Another heap contains exactly five cards. It is the only heap which has that number—all other heaps have either more or less than five cards. Should this particular heap be selected, the wizard says:

"The 'five' heap. Your heap is the only one with five cards." He counts the cards in that heap and also the cards in the other heaps. But he turns none of the heaps face upward. This artifice is very convincing.

A third heap can also be made to appear as the "five" heap. It contains just four cards—three aces and a two spot. If this heap is selected, the magician picks it up and holds it face downward. One by one, he deals the cards face up on the table, counting the spots: "One, two, three and two make five!"

He then deals the other heaps the same way, showing that each has cards totalling more than five. When he picks up the heap with four fives, he simply deals two cards face up saying: "Five—ten—that's more than five already!"

When these heaps are laid out, the heap with the four fives should be in the center, flanked by the other two heaps just mentioned, the magician knowing the position of each individual heap. There are two more heaps to consider. These are the end heaps. Each consists of eight or nine indifferent cards.

Should one of these heaps be designated, the magician tells the chooser to leave it on the table. The paper is opened. The message is read.

"The 'five' heap," says the magician. "I told you that we count the heaps one, two, three, four, five—from left to right. That makes your heap number five—the 'five' heap."

It makes no difference which end heap is chosen. If the one selected is at the performer's right, he counts the heaps himself, running his hand from left to right. If the selected heap is at the performer's left, he orders the chooser to count to the correct heap —one, two, three, four, five—and the count ends on the selected heap.

It is advisable to call for this counting before the message is read. That makes the choice unmistakably five and the spectator picks up the heap while the paper is being unfolded. The magician then sweeps the other four heaps together and replaces them with the pack.

By having these cards set in order in the pack, the trick may be presented in a very smart fashion. It is a great improvement on old ideas of this order and can be turned into a very puzzling problem. It depends entirely upon presentation and requires no skill whatever.

4. DOUBLE DISCOVERY

A person takes a pack of cards from the performer. He cuts it in two heaps. He removes a cluster of cards from the lower half. He counts those cards and notes the bottom card of the group—say seven cards with the six of spades on the bottom. He must not take more than thirteen cards.

He is instructed to place the group with the chosen card on the other half of the pack. The performer's back is turned while this goes on. When the operation is completed, the magician turns around and picks up the pack, putting the top half on top.

Now he deals cards faces down, in a sort of circle. He does this with about twenty cards. Running his hand around, he suddenly turns a card face up. It is a seven spot. The performer announces that there were seven cards in the spectator's group. Instantly, the performer turns up another card. It is the six of spades, the card noted by the person.

In doing this trick, the magician first states that jack counts as eleven, queen as twelve and king as thirteen. On top of the pack he has thirteen cards arranged in this order, from the top: king, queen, jack, ten, nine, eight, seven, six, five, four, three, two, ace.

Note that the group taken by the spectator goes on these cards. It does not matter how many cards the group contains. The fourteenth card from the top will indicate, by its value, the number of cards put on by the spectator.

Thus the spectator takes seven cards, the bottom of his group being the six of spades, which he remembers. The performer deals from fifteen to twenty cards in a rough circle. He turns up the fourteenth card, counting around the circle and it is a seven spot.

That gives him a clue to the location of the spectator's noted card. It must be the one that was dealt seventh in the circle. Quickly going around the circle, the magician turns up the seventh card to reveal it as the selected one.

Suppose the spectator had ten cards in his group, with the five of clubs on the bottom. The fourteenth card, when turned up by the conjuror, would be a ten spot. Counting to the tenth card in the circle, the performer would discover the five of clubs.

Immediately after revealing the selected card, the magician should mix the cards of the circle as he prepares to gather them up. This destroys any arrangement and leaves the spectators wondering, even if they do happen to see the faces of the cards.

5. THE CARD FORETOLD

There are various card tricks that involve predictions; this is one of the simplest yet most effective. It may be performed with an ordinary pack although the magician must be set beforehand.

A pack of cards is divided into two heaps which are shuffled together in dovetail fashion—a careful, legitimate shuffle. Something is written on a sheet of paper which is dropped in a glass or placed in the card-case.

Turning the pack face up, the magician states that he will carefully separate the reds from the blacks. Someone else may do this if desired—but the magician requests that it be done exactly, dealing each red or black card as it comes.

Thus two piles are obtained. A person is asked to choose either the red heap or the black heap. Suppose red is taken. The magician gives the cards value from one to thirteen—ace, one; jack, eleven; queen, twelve; king, thirteen. He asks all to note that if two cards are taken from the red heap, their value may indicate any number from one to twenty-six: two aces equaling two; two kings, twenty-six; other pairs, numbers in between. This fact is readily understood.

So the magician asks the spectator to cut the red pack at any point and to add the values of the two cards above and below the cut. These two values are to designate a card in the black heap—counting down from the top.

The cut is made. We will suppose that a five and a nine appear. They total fourteen. A spectator counts down fourteen in the black heap. The card is the ace of clubs. The folded paper is opened. It bears the name "ace of clubs"!

Now for the simple method. The magician first separates the red cards from the blacks—long before he shows the trick. He arranges the red cards thus:

King, ace, queen, two, jack, three, ten, four, nine, five, eight, six, seven, seven, eight, six, nine, five, ten, four, jack, three, queen, two, king, ace.

There is no arrangement of the black heap. The magician simply notes the fourteenth card from the bottom. That is the card upon which the choice is to fall—in this instance, the ace of clubs.

When the pack is introduced, the two heaps are segregated as described—one color being upon the other. The magician turns the faces of the cards toward himself; spreading them slightly, he separates the pack so that he has the reds in one hand and the blacks in the other. He then proceeds with the dovetail shuffle—or lets some spectator perform that action.

The result: reds and blacks are intermingled, but the reds still retain their original order and the ace of clubs is still fourteen from the bottom—among the blacks. So when the pack is turned face up and the cards are separated one by one into two heaps, the peculiar arrangement of the reds remains comparatively the same. The ace of clubs now becomes fourteen from the top in the black heap.

The arrangement of the reds is important for this reason. No matter where that heap is cut, the cards above and below the cut will add to a total of either thirteen or fourteen! If the total is thirteen, the magician asks someone to remove thirteen cards from the top of the black heap and to look at the next card. If the total is fourteen, he tells the person to look at the fourteenth card from the top of the black heap. In either instance, the action seems to abide by the magician's promise—to take the card at the number designated by the red totals. Also, in either instance, the card consulted is the ace of clubs.

The magician has, of course, written his mysterious words early in the trick—just after introducing the pack. So everyone is due for amazement when the paper is opened and seen to bear the words ace of clubs.

There is just one other point. The magician, after the cards are separated, allows the spectator to select either heap—reds or blacks. This is simply a bit of by-play. Since both heaps are to be used, the magician cannot go wrong. If reds are taken, he uses them to ascertain a number in the black heap. If blacks are taken, he states that he has predicted a black card and merely uses the red heap to pick a number at random.

6. PASSE PASSE CARDS

This wonderful effect is now explained with certain modifications that make it a most excellent mystery for performance anywhere. It can be done in the parlor or on the stage—with small cards or with giant cards.

All that is needed is two packs with different white-margined backs—preferably a red pack and a blue pack. Also two drinking glasses (stands if giant cards are used) and some rubber bands.

Taking the red pack of cards, the magician has one selected. It is replaced in a cluster of about twelve cards which the magician removes from the bottom of the deck. Encircled with rubber bands, this packet is placed in a glass.

Next a card is similarly taken from the blue pack and is replaced in a cluster of about twelve cards taken from the bottom of the pack. This group is also girded with rubber bands and it goes in the other glass.

To show the location of each heap, a card is removed from each group and set back forward in front of the glass in which the group is located. On the right, a red card shows the red packet; on the left, a blue card shows the blue packet.

The magician takes both packets, explaining that the rubber bands now make it impossible to remove a card from the group without considerable difficulty. He tosses the groups in the air. He picks them up or catches them. He puts the red group in its glass —the blue group in its glass. Now comes the baffling finish. The glasses are given to the spectators. Among the red cards is found the blue-backed card that was selected from the blue pack! Among the blue cards is discovered the red-backed card that was taken from the red pack!

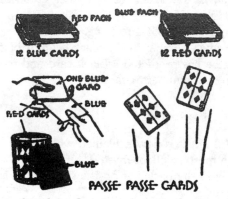

Arrangement of packs and various stages in the Passe Passe Card Trick.

A wonderful trick, yet quite simple and easy to do. Just a bit of quick preparation is necessary. Before performing, take one dozen red cards from the red pack and put them on the bottom of the blue pack. Likewise take a dozen blue cards and put them on the bottom of the red pack.

Important: The bottom card of each group should be the same —say the six of diamonds. Then the performer is ready to work. If he is using his own cards, he should have the packs in their cases.

A card is chosen from the red pack. In spreading the pack for a selection, the magician does not spread the bottom cards. Hence the blue backs do not come into view. After the card is taken, the magician spreads the faces of the pack toward the spectators. This enables him to see the backs. He draws off all the blue cards from the bottom, but keeps one red card on top of them. He squares these cards and holds them faces down for the insertion of the chosen card. The single red-backed card makes it seem as though the group consisted entirely of red-backed cards.

The procedure with the blue pack is exactly the same. The red-backed cards at the bottom are not spread when a blue card is selected. But in spreading the pack faces front, the red-backed cards are drawn off beneath a blue-backed card.

The chosen blue card goes into the little squared-up heap. It appears to be going into a packet of bona fide blue cards.

Each packet is girded with rubber bands and placed in a glass, with the bottom card facing the audience. To point out the location of red and blue, the magician takes the top card from each heap and sets it in front of the glass. This is a clever idea. It disposes of the extra card in each group.

One packet is taken in each hand—faces of the cards toward the audience. Each packet appears the same, because the facing cards are identical. Each is a six of diamonds. Now the groups are brought together and tossed. When they come down, no one knows which is which. But the magician shows the backs and calmly places the red-backed group in the glass indicated by the red card, while the blue-backed packet goes in the glass indicated by the blue card.

No one realizes the subtle change that has taken place. Yet the performer announces that the simple toss in the air has caused each selected card to leave its own group and pass into the other! Wonderful, if true.

It appears to be true when the spectators take the packets from the glasses. The blue-backed card is with the reds; the red-backed card is in the midst of the blues. Not a clue to the secret remains.

7 . CARDS AND ENVELOPES

A very surprising mystery. Three selected cards apparently leave an envelope and pass into a group of cards contained in another envelope.

The magician begins by dealing sixteen cards from a pack.

These sixteen cards are counted by a spectator. The magician puts them in an envelope, which is sealed and marked.

Next, sixteen more cards are counted faces down; they are spread on the table and three cards are turned up and noted by spectators. The magician shuffles these cards and puts them in the second envelope, which is also sealed.

The first surprise comes when nineteen cards are discovered in the first envelope. Opening the second envelope and counting the cards therein, only thirteen are found. Then the nineteen group is counted faces up and the chosen cards are discovered in it!

The secret depends upon two groups of sixteen cards that are exactly alike. This means that the magician must use his own pack, having his special arrangement made up with the aid of a duplicate pack. The groups of sixteen cards are on top of the pack. Thus when the magician counts off sixteen cards and then another group of sixteen, he is forming two heaps that are identical. But the cards are faces down so no one knows this fact.

Beneath one envelope—which we will call A—are three odd cards, lying faces down. The envelope and the cards overlap the edge of the table slightly. Now, the performer must secretly add those three cards to the sixteen which he intends to put into envelope A.

There are two ways of doing this. First Method: Lay the sixteen cards faces down on the envelope, drawing out the envelope at almost the same moment. Second Method: Pick up the envelope with the three cards beneath it and let it rest momentarily above the sixteen cards. The three odd cards are allowed to fall upon the sixteen, which are a trifle disarranged.

Either method works and the upshot is that nineteen cards go into envelope A, despite the fact that sixteen were carefully counted at the outset.

Three cards are now selected from the other group—the cards that are to go into envelope B. Note that these cards are turned up from among the sixteen, so no one becomes acquainted with any of the cards other than the selected ones.

Upon shuffling this bunch of sixteen, the magician holds the group in his right hand, thumb at one end, fingers at the other—

the cards faces down beneath the hand. With the aid of the left hand, he forms a slight space at the bottom of the group so that three cards are detached from the others.

He picks up envelope B and holds it with the flap extended— the face of the envelope downward. He moves the envelope toward his right hand, the extended flap pointing like an arrow.

In sliding the cards into the envelope, it is a simple matter to insert the point of the flap between the bulk of thirteen cards and the three odd cards that are separated beneath. The result is that only thirteen cards actually go into envelope B. The rest go beneath. The left fingers, under the envelope, help the odd cards into position and hold them there.

This envelope is held momentarily over the pack of cards, which is lying—somewhat disarranged—on the table. The left fingers release their cards, so that the odd cards fall on the table. Envelope B is then sealed.

Now for the action, the important part of the trick being ended. The performer commands the selected cards to pass from envelope B to envelope A. Upon opening envelope A, nineteen cards are discovered, being counted faces down. Envelope B is opened. Only thirteen cards—counted faces down.

Picking up the pack, the performer holds it in his left hand, while the right holds the thirteen cards. Spectators are told to turn the nineteen cards faces up and look for the three selected cards. During this search, the magician adds the three top cards of the pack to the thirteen in his right hand and transfers all to the bottom of the pack. He quietly counts off thirteen—to be ready in case anyone asks to see the thirteen cards from envelope B.

To make this quick, those thirteen cards can be previously bent upward in the center so they can be lifted off the pack when needed. Generally the spectators are so surprised to find the chosen cards with the nineteen that the trick can be ended there. Due to the duplication of the packets, the selected cards must be in the nineteen heap.

8. ONE, TWO, THREE

The magician holds the ace, deuce, and trey in the form of a fan, the ace at the front, and all cards of the same suit, say spades. The cards are squared and placed face down on top of the pack.

Now, they are carefully dealt in a row, all face down: trey, deuce, ace, from left to right. The magician states he will drive the cards up and down through the entire pack, in one, two, three order.

Bam! He slaps the pack down on the ace. An instant later, he turns up the top card. It is the ace of spades! He tosses the ace aside, places the two of spades face down on top of the pack and strikes the pack with his fist. He turns the pack over to show that the deuce is on the bottom!

Tossing the deuce aside, he drops the pack face down on the remaining card, the trey. He turns up the top card of the pack and there is the three of spades—as big as life! It is tossed aside with the other two members of the magic trio.

No duplicates; just a simple subterfuge, plus a brisk routine. In showing the original fan, have an odd card squared behind the trey, so there are actually *four* cards, not just three. When the cards are squared and dealt from the pack, they will be in the order: odd, trey, deuce—the ace remaining on top of the pack.

Spectators suppose that the ace, deuce, and trey are actually on the table. The magician drops the pack on the supposed ace— really the deuce—and shows the true ace on top of the pack. He puts the supposed deuce—really the trey—on top of the pack and shows that the deuce has "gone" to the bottom. He drops the pack on the supposed trey—really the odd card—and promptly shows that the trey is on top of the pack.

9. YANKEE DOODLE

Similar to a spelling trick. A card is selected and people are told to sing "Yankee Doodle" while the magician deals cards in time to the song. At the finish, he turns up the chosen card.

In spreading the pack for the selection, count the cards to yourself until you reach fifteen. Hold a break at that point for replacement of the chosen card, so it will be the sixteenth from the top.*

Hit the beats of the song as you deal, thus:

> "Yan-*kee*--Doo-*dle*--came *to--town*
> Rid-*ing*--on *a--po--ny*
> He *stuck*--a *feath*--er *in*--his *hat*
> And *called*--it *mac*--a *ron--ee.*"

The song ends on the sixteenth beat and the chosen card is turned up as the magical surprise.

10. NUMERO

Tell a spectator to deal a small number of cards secretly. Suppose that he deals eight. Tell him to deal the same number on those already dealt: $8 + 8 = 16$.

Now tell him to deal ten more cards on the pile: $16 + 10 = 26$. He is then to deal the cards into two heaps and discard either group. That leaves him with thirteen cards.

All this is unseen by the performer who now tells the person to deal off his original number (eight) and retain the rest: $13 - 8 = 5$.

The spectator concentrates on the cards he holds and the magician catches the thought, suddenly saying: "You have exactly five cards!"

He will always have five cards, because it is half the number he was told to add; namely, ten. Whatever the spectator's own number, it works out the same. Try it and see.

If he is told to add twelve, he will wind up with six. If he adds sixteen, he will finish with eight. So the trick can be varied whenever you want to repeat it.

---

* This is the same method used with the "Simplicity Speller" (page 69) except for a variation in the card count.

11. THE RED CARDS

The magician hands a person a slip of paper bearing a prediction. He then gives the spectator a choice of two envelopes, each containing some playing cards. The prediction is opened and it states: "You will take the red cards."

When the envelopes are opened, the prediction is fulfilled. The spectator finds he actually took the red cards! The cards from his envelope are spread face up and they are all red—hearts and diamonds; while those in the other envelope are blacks—clubs and spades.

What if the person should choose the wrong envelope? He can't, for a very simple reason. In setting up the trick, the magician takes the red set (hearts and diamonds) from a pack with a *blue back*. The black cards (spades and clubs) are taken from a *red-backed* pack.

If someone picks the envelope containing the spades and clubs, the magician turns over the envelopes before opening them and when he removes the cards, he spreads them *face down*. So the spectator finds the "red" cards (red-backers) in his envelope, exactly as the prediction stated.

In one case, the chooser is shown only the faces of the cards; in the other, just the backs. So the magician must open the envelopes and spread the cards himself. Immediately afterward, he should gather them—face up or face down, as the case may be—and put them in his pocket.

That swift sequel in no way detracts from the trick, as the whole action is very convincing. It's just a case of remembering how the cards lie in the envelopes and handling them accordingly. The trick can not be repeated before the same audience, as a different "choice" of envelopes would give away the subterfuge.

Chapter VIII

BLACKSTONE'S SLEIGHT-OF-HAND WITH CARDS

In a great number of card tricks, a chosen card is taken from the pack, returned; and after the pack is shuffled, the card is discovered by the performer, in some mysterious fashion.

In order to do this, it is essential that the card be controlled by the magician, and it has always been customary to make use of a sleight known as the "pass" or "shift."

Now the "pass" is a difficult movement to acquire. It is nothing more than an invisible cut, executed at close range. When a card is replaced in the center of the pack, the performer invisibly cuts the pack, thus bringing the chosen card to the top or bottom as he desires.

With the majority of card performers, the "pass" is not invisible; with others, it is a suspicious movement; with all it is unnecessary. Why, when a single card is to be removed from the center of the pack and placed on the top or bottom, should anyone go to the difficulty of moving half the pack?

With some expert magicians, the "pass" works in practice; but it is wrong in theory. Furthermore, it is seldom effective unless the hands immediately move into a shuffle, which is a natural action following the return of a chosen card. The method of controlling a chosen card that is described here is direct, effective and easy of accomplishment, utilizing the shuffle as a natural follow-up. It has mystified magicians, and with it the beginner can work wonders after very little practice.

1. BLACKSTONE'S CARD CONTROL

Spread the pack between the hands, and allow someone to select a card. While this is being done, square the cards and hold them firmly in the left hand, thumb above, fingers below.

With the right hand, bend up the outer ends of the cards, and

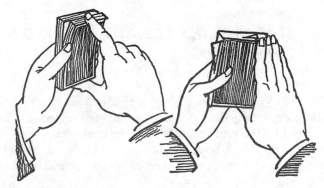

LEFT: Riffling the pack.
RIGHT: Pushing the chosen card to the left.

allow them to fall in quick succession. This is known as the "riffle." Stop the "riffle," or let the cards fall slowly, so that the chosen card may be returned.

Now comes the important movement. The pressure of the left hand prevents the card from going entirely into the pack. With the right hand, push the card in, but turn it slightly to the left, so that it goes in at an angle. The outer left end of the card will project slightly when the outer right is flush with the pack.

This is the cue for the left thumb to gently slide the top cards of the pack to the left, so that they hide the projecting corner. The pack appears quite normal.

The shuffle follows immediately. The right hand comes from beneath, and the fingers grip the outer end of the pack, while the thumb presses against the inner end.

The left thumb draws off one or more of the top cards; and

the left forefinger, hidden beneath them, catches the projecting corner of the chosen card, and carries it along.

Thus the chosen card becomes the bottom one of those which have been drawn off. The shuffle is continued by drawing off more cards with the left thumb, and letting them fall on those first removed. Proceed thus until the entire pack has been drawn off in shuffles, and the bottom card will be the one that was chosen.

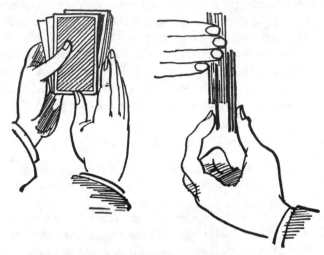

LEFT: Sliding top cards over chosen card.
RIGHT: Drawing out chosen card in shuffle.

This movement is simple and natural—and for that reason it is effective. Yet there are certain errors which must be avoided.

First: some difficulty may be experienced in drawing out the chosen card easily. This can be overcome by moistening the forefinger slightly; also by lifting up with the forefinger so as to relieve any pressure on the card.

Second: there will be a tendency to draw off all the cards above the chosen one in a single group. This ruins the effectiveness of the movement. To counteract this tendency, press the upper half of the pack very firmly between the right thumb and fingers. This makes it necessary to draw out the chosen card.

The beauty of this sleight lies in the fact that the chosen card actually goes in the center of the pack; and the shuffle follows in a natural manner. The passage of the selected card is absolutely invisible, being completely covered by the cards above; and sharp-eyed observers begin to look for some action *after* the essential part of the maneuver has been accomplished.

Speed is not necessary; but smoothness should be acquired. Hesitancy will cause suspicion, even though the sleight is indetectible. The movement of the cards to the left should begin immediately after the chosen card has been inserted.

In shuffling, hold the cards close to the horizontal, or turn so that the backs of the cards are toward the spectators. A slight tilt to the left is natural; but if the vertical position is preferred, precaution must be taken to keep the bottom card from showing.

2. FALSE SHUFFLE SYSTEM

The false shuffle is the movement whereby the performer apparently shuffles the pack thoroughly, yet keeps the chosen card in a desired position.

In connection with the system of card control, the best method is a shuffle that constantly transfers the chosen card from bottom to top, and vice versa. This is actually a genuine shuffle; hence cannot excite suspicion.

To bring the card to the top, utilize the same method of shuffling, peeling off a few cards from the top with the left thumb. But when the bottom of the pack is reached, draw off cards one by one. Result: the chosen card will end on top.

To bring it to the bottom again, merely draw off the top card alone, and shuffle the others on it. Moistening the thumb often helps in this action.

Several cards are controlled as follows: Bring the first selected card to the bottom, and either leave it there, or shuffle it to the top and back to the bottom.

Then the second selected card is returned to the pack.

Bring it to the bottom by the card control; but as the shuffle is concluded, run the cards one by one so that the first selected card remains on top.

Then place the left thumb on top of the pack and the fingers beneath, and draw off the top and bottom cards together. Shuffle the rest of the pack on them. The two selected cards will be at the bottom. They can be brought to the top in the usual fashion, for they are treated singly at the finish of the shuffle.

If a third selected card is used—or a fourth—have the cards previously selected at the bottom, and proceed exactly as with the second card. With three cards under control, one will come on the bottom and two on top.

To bring all to the bottom, draw off the top and bottom cards as one; draw the next top card on to them; and continue the shuffle. With four under control, there will be three on top; so bring two off singly.

Experiment with the cards will show that any number of cards can be controlled in this manner. The performer must keep his mind on the cards, and practice the various movements; but throughout the actions will always be natural.

It will be observed that the card control and the shuffle system work together. One is virtually a part of the other. All awkward movements are avoided, and in the apparent action of mixing the cards, the performer can keep them on the top or bottom of the pack as he prefers.

With a group of chosen cards on the bottom, shuffle naturally until the group is reached; then finish by single runs, a card at a time. The same group can be brought to the bottom by running the top cards one at a time and then shuffling the rest of the pack on them.

3 . THE END SHUFFLE

In addition to the usual shuffle, described above, the "end shuffle" should be cultivated. The pack is held in the left hand, which is palm upward, fingers at the left of the pack and the thumb at the right. The pack is in a horizontal position.

With the thumb and second finger of the right hand, pull a

clump of cards from the center of the pack, drawing the cards toward the body. Drop them on the pack, and immediately draw out a smaller cluster of cards, placing them on top; and continue this operation several times, the group of cards dwindling with each withdrawal.

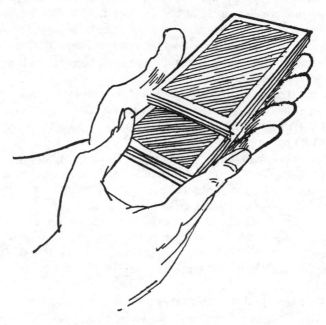

This can be done quite rapidly, and makes a very convincing shuffle. It also serves as a false shuffle when the chosen cards are on the bottom, for the lower cards of the pack are not disturbed, no matter how often the shuffle may be repeated.

This shuffle also serves another important purpose. The "pass" was not employed merely to bring chosen cards to the top of the pack; it was sometimes used to bring a desired card back to the center, from either the top or the bottom.

Now with the "end shuffle," this is very easily done. The shuffle is virtually continuous, done time and again; and in concluding the shuffle, the right hand merely draws out the bottom half of the pack, and drops it on top, thus bringing the bottom card of the pack to the center. By dropping the section at an angle, a slight step is formed, so that the pack may be separated at that point.

4. TO FORCE A CARD

Making a person take a certain card from the pack is called the "force," and it is a useful accomplishment. It has been described in many works on magic, and the instructions invariably say to note the bottom card, bring it to the center by the "pass" and proceed.

The author's plan is to sight the bottom card by turning the bottom of the pack toward himself. Then he begins the "end shuffle," apparently mixing the cards, and finishes by a cut that brings the known card to the center of the pack.

At this point, the section placed on top of the pack should be set well to the right, so that it rests on the third and fourth fingers

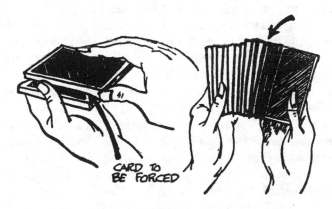

CARD TO
BE FORCED

of the left hand. The pack drops flat on the left palm, and the thumbs of both hands begin a spreading process so that a person may select a card.

The theory of the "force" is to spread the cards in such a manner that the chooser will naturally take the desired card. This is accomplished by timing the speed of the cards as they go from left to right, so that the particular card reaches the person's hand just at the instant he is ready to draw a card.

The most important element in the "force" is that of surprise. If the spectator does not suspect the performer's purpose, the chance of success is very great.

Most magicians time the "force" according to the spectator. In some instances they are very leisurely. As it is a bad plan to slow down or speed up to a noticeable extent, once the cards are being spread, the spectator not infrequently takes a card very close to the desired one, and the "force" fails. This is not alarming, because the card can be "forced" on another person; nevertheless, a sure-fire "force" is something to be desired, and I shall explain just such a method.

Do not start to spread the cards until the spectator is virtually ready to take one. Inject a spirit of action into the procedure. Then begin to spread the cards, quite rapidly—so rapidly indeed that the person cannot easily take one.

At the same time, keep the hands moving so that the pack is always going away from him, moving here and there, and making it impossible for him to get the card. Just as the chosen card arrives, reverse the process, suddenly stopping the retreating policy and letting the pack come suddenly toward the person. At the instant he grasps, the chosen card is ready for him—the spreading has ceased; and he gets the card you want him to have.

The card to be "forced" should be quite a bit below the center of the pack; and if this plan is followed, the "force" will not only be sure, but will be quite as effective as a leisurely system.

In brief, the spectator is ready to take the card all along, but he can't get it until the performer wishes. Yet the movement must be natural. The spectator, in his eagerness, will not realize that the performer is keeping the cards just out of his reach, and he will snatch the proper card with pleasure.

In actuality, the performer spreads the cards until he reaches the proper one and then thrusts it into the spectator's hand; but in performing, this should be done artfully. The magician must seem indifferent about the matter; his speed must seem his natural method; he must not apparently draw the pack away nor thrust it forward.

Whenever a "force" fails through any cause, the card should be "forced" on another person. Then the first card taken may be used in another trick, by means of the card control.

Summary of Preceding Sleights

The various movements just described constitute a new variety of card work that is in opposition to most accepted systems. The "pass" is avoided. A chosen card is preferably kept on the bottom instead of on the top. The constant transfer from bottom to top eliminates tricky shuffles.

The "pass" whenever necessary is replaced by an open cut in the course of the "end shuffle." The "force" is rapid instead of leisurely. By conforming with these methods, effective results will be obtained.

5. THE SECOND DEAL

The "second deal" is a sleight neglected by magicians; yet it is extremely useful. It consists in apparently dealing the cards in a regular manner from the top of the pack; but actually retaining the top card all the while.

To accomplish this, lay the pack across the left palm, so that the left thumb may rest lightly along one edge. Hold the hand toward the body, so that the left thumb extends directly outward.

Now practice dealing the cards one by one; drawing the top card directly to the right with the right thumb, which touches the card at the outer right corner. As each card clears the pack, the right fingers grip it from beneath, and carry it away.

This is the natural, simple method of dealing that is to be simulated with the "second deal."

Press the tip of the left thumb lightly on the top card and move the thumb slowly toward the body. You will observe that the top card will move inward, as though pivoted in the form of the left thumb—the outer left corner of the card will retain its position.

By advancing the thumb, the card will resume its former place. This must be done very lightly, in order to move the top card independently.

When the outer right corner of the top card has been drawn inward about half an inch, you will find it an easy matter to pull

The position of the hands in the "Second Deal."

out the second card with the aid of the right thumb—exactly as you would normally draw off the top card.

As the right hand draws the card clear, advance the left thumb again so that the top card resumes its normal position. This is the basis of the second deal.

But in actual practice, the left thumb should draw in the top card as little as possible—not much more than one-eighth of an inch. This is because the left thumb serves to hide the top card, and no clue should be given to movement of the top card.

If both thumbs are slightly dampened, the sleight will become much less difficult; for less pressure will be necessary on the part of the left; and the right will be able to pull away the second card even though it touches only the edge of the card at the corner.

The position of the left thumb is important. It should rest at the extreme edge of the top card, so that the end of the card will not be in view beneath the thumb. The left fingers also assist by curling up against the side of the pack, thus holding the deck square. Each card that the right hand deals slides over the tips of the left fingers.

This sleight is quite easy to learn; but it is one that requires considerable practice to perfect. The performer must learn to execute it with constant precision, and he must also learn to deal the cards with the rapidity that is customary in dealing cards normally from the top of the pack.

A natural motion of the hands also serves to facilitate the sleight as well as making it more deceptive. The left hand should approach the right while the left thumb is drawing back the top card. The moment that the hands meet, the deal of the second card begins, the left hand going away as the right hand removes the card. The hands should perform their functions automatically, the eyes of the performer being on the cards that have been dealt, or gazing toward the spectators. Ordinary dealing is a very easy process; and the magician should endeavor to make the "second deal" appear just as easy.

6. THE CHANGES

The sleights just given are new, and little-known. I shall explain two old sleights for the sake of completeness. These are the "changes."

(A) *The "Bottom Change"*

LEFT: Beginning the "Bottom Change."
RIGHT: The exchange of the cards.

Hold a card between the first and second fingers of the right hand. The pack lies in the left, as though ready for a deal—the left thumb on top.

As the right hand approaches the left, all the left fingers except the forefinger are lowered, so the single card may be placed between them and the forefinger.

At the same instant, the left thumb pushes the top card of the pack to the right, so that it may be taken between the thumb and forefinger of the right hand. These two motions, the deposit of one card on the bottom of the pack and the removal of the top card take place simultaneously.

(B) The "Top Change"

This is the reverse of the "bottom change." The single card is held between the right thumb and forefinger. The left hand

LEFT: The beginning of the "Top Change."
RIGHT: The exchange of the cards.

pushes the top card to the right. As the right hand lays its card on the pack, the forefinger and second finger simultaneously grip the top card of the pack and carry it away.

The "changes" when executed, require a good misdirection. The right hand holds a card and thrusts it toward a spectator while the performer inquires "Your card?" As he awaits an answer, and the person's eyes meet his, he brings the card back to the pack and makes the change, the left hand withdrawing while the right comes slowly forward.

Or the performer may show a card to a person on his right; and as he turns to his left, the hands meet in front of the body long enough for the "change" to be made—a fraction of a second. Never look at the hands while executing one of these sleights.

7. CARD TRICKS WITH SLEIGHTS

With the various sleights at his disposal, the magician can perform many excellent tricks. A few are enumerated here.

(A) *The Self-Turning Card*

Bring a chosen card to the top of the pack. Lay the pack on the palm of the right hand, crosswise; with the thumb over the center. Push the top card slightly forward with the thumb and tilt it up a bit with the tip of the second finger.

Then slide the cards along the table. The top card will be turned over by the pressure of the air, and will appear face up in the midst of the spread out pack.

(B) A Double Mistake

Have two cards selected and bring them both to the top. Show one card to the person on your right—the card that he did not choose. He will state that it is not his card. Turn to the left, making the "top change." Show the card you now have to the person on your left—he will not recognize it either.

Turn slowly to the first person, and let him see the card again. To his surprise it has become the card he chose. While he is admitting that he was mistaken before, turn to the second person, executing the "bottom change" (or the "top change") and let him see the card again. He will have to admit that it is also his card!

(C) Any Number

This is one of the most effective of card tricks. Bring a chosen card to the top; and ask for any small number. Suppose "eight" is given. Deal off seven cards with the "second deal"; then turn up the top card at number eight. It will be the chosen one, appearing at the number desired.

This can be done without the second deal, by simply counting off eight cards one by one, drawing each one on the card before, thus reversing their order. The eighth card will not be the chosen one. In replacing the eight on the pack, the chosen card naturally becomes the eighth; so you riffle the pack and let the chooser count eight for himself. He will find the card there.

An improvement on this version is to count off the eight, and drop the eighth face down on the table. While people are looking at it, return the other seven to the pack; but let the bottom card of the group rest for a moment on the tips of the left fingers, while the right fingers flip it face up beneath the other cards of the group. The card on the table is put back on the pack. When a spectator counts off eight, he finds the chosen card there—face up.

(D) *All Alike*

Let a person select a card. Bring it to the bottom of the pack. Force the same card on a second person; bring it to the bottom and force on a third person. Then bring the card to the top. You lay this card on the table and state that it is one of the three cards chosen; that any one of the three who really believes it is his card will find that it is.

Turn the card up, and all persons will recognize their card. This can be varied by first showing a card from the center of the pack. None will acknowledge it. Make a change, and lay the card on the table. This time all will be forced to acknowledge it.

(E) *Self-Revealing Card*

This is a nice little finish to a card trick. A chosen card is brought to the top and the pack is laid on the right hand. Draw the top card slightly inward so that one corner presses into the base of the thumb; and the other corner comes beneath the tip of the little finger. Press downward with the little finger and the card will mysteriously rise to an upright position.

8. THE KNIFE IN THE PACK

This is a new trick—a very clever effect. Holding a pack horizontally between the tips of his left thumb and forefinger, the magician inserts a knife into the center of the pack.

He immediately announces the name of the card above the knife. He places his right forefinger on top of the pack and lifts up all the cards above the knife, showing the card he named.

The trick may be repeated; and spectators may insert the knife. But the performer, before he lifts the cards will always name the card correctly.

The Method: Use a table-knife with a bright blade. When the knife has been inserted, tilt the pack very slightly to the right. At the same instant, tilt the knife blade slightly to the left, moving it so that it comes directly under the inner left corner of the pack.

You will immediately catch a reflection of the index corner of the card above the knife. That is the card you name, before you lift up the upper half of the pack.

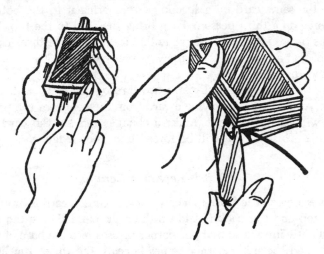

If the pack is held high, so that it is almost on a level with the eyes, the tilting motions are virtually unnecessary. The weight of the knife will bend down the lower half of the cards a bit, and you will catch the reflection easily.

With practice, this trick can be accomplished easily, and with regular precision.

9. THE SPECTATORS' TRICK

The ambition of every magician is to allow a spectator to shuffle a pack, and have another person take a card from it and re-place it, shuffling the pack for himself—after which the magician finds the chosen card.

This seeming miracle of card magic is quite possible, with the use of a "one way" pack—or "single enders" as they are sometimes termed. Such a pack consists of cards which have a design on the back that is different at one end from the other. Obviously, if the cards are arranged with the patterns all one way, a card that is turned around can be easily discovered by looking through the pack.

Armed with such a pack, with the cards all pointing in one direction, the trick may be undertaken. Let a spectator shuffle the cards—taking care that he does not "riffle" the ends together, but merely uses the ordinary overhand shuffle. Then tell him to spread the cards and let a person take one.

While the pack is still held, tell him to turn his back so that the chooser may insert his card without anyone seeing where it goes. This automatically turns the ends of the cards the other way; so when the chosen card is inserted, the pack may be shuffled normally; yet the magician can immediately find the card by looking through the pack for the one that is reversed.

Most expensive cards are "single enders"; but the patterns are too obvious. There are two styles of "Bicycle" cards—the "Emblem Back" and the "Wheel Back" that are excellent one-way cards, as the pattern does not reveal this peculiarity to the average person.

10. THE TRAVELING DEUCE

This is an old trick with a surprising finish that is quite new. A deuce of diamonds is inserted at various positions near the center of the pack, but it always appears on the top or the bottom.

Place the deuce on top of the pack to begin; and see that the trey or three-spot of the same suit is located fourth.

Show the deuce; execute the "top change," and insert the card which people believe to be the deuce in the center of the pack. Naturally, it passes to the top.

Then make the "bottom change" and push the card into the center; this time the deuce turns up at the bottom.

Turn away for an instant to pick up a table-knife. In so doing, slide the deuce under the trey which is on top of the pack.

Insert the knife beneath the top card, so that it runs diagonally across the center of the card from right to left. Press the forefinger on top of the card, and raise it so all can see the face.

The knife blade, passing across both index corners and the center spot of the trey, make it appear to be the deuce. There is no mistake this time; everyone sees the card pushed into the center of the pack with the aid of the knife; and all are convinced it is the deuce. Remove the knife and insert it diagonally under the

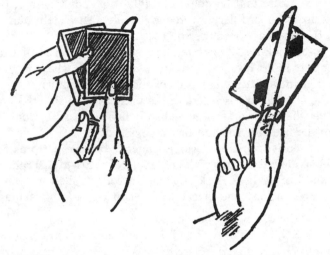

Lifting the three spot to make it appear as a deuce.

top card from right to left, this time. Turn up the card on the knife and reveal the deuce—the index corners being unconcealed.

This is a very convincing procedure that is sure to prove mystifying.

11. THE TEN CARD TRICK

Two heaps of ten cards—from one heap, three cards pass invisibly, one at a time. They appear in the other heap. Both heaps are held by spectators. This is always a good trick; and the author's favorite sleight is absolutely indetectible.

This trick is one of the specialties of Nate Leipzig, the famous card manipulator.

Let someone count ten cards on your left hand—one by one.

This person stands on your left. Then you place a borrowed handkerchief over your extended left arm, and allow someone to count ten cards on to your right hand, the counter standing on your right.

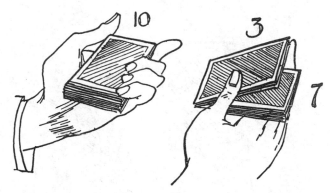

While this is taking place, slide the three top cards of the left hand on to the tips of the left fingers.

Turn your left side toward the man on the right, and request him to remove the handkerchief from the arm. This brings the left hand close to the right, and slightly above it, as the left arm is raised a bit. The three loose cards are immediately slid on to the cards in the right hand.

Face the audience the instant the handkerchief is removed, swinging the hands wide apart. Tell the man on your right to "find the center of the handkerchief—which is in the middle." Then give him the cards from your right hand and see that he wraps them tightly in the cloth.

Flip the cards in your left hand, and state that one has passed from that group, into the handkerchief. To prove this, you count the cards.

Here you must utilize a simple sleight known as the "false count." Draw the top card of the heap away in the right hand, counting "one." Place it on the second card of the heap and count "two," drawing both cards away. Do the same on "three"; but on the counts of "four" and "five" do not remove any cards from the heap. Then proceed "six, seven, eight, nine," in normal fashion.

State that another card will pass into the handkerchief. Flip the cards, and count them again, this time making the "false count" on but one occasion, thus counting eight.

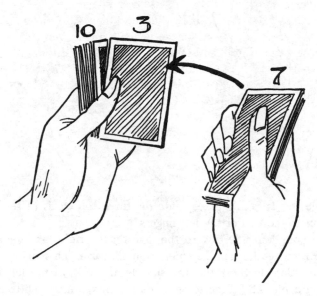

Place the cards in the hands of the man on your left, and give them another flip. Tell him to count them. He finds only seven. The man with the handkerchief finds that he has thirteen cards!

Note: If difficulty is experienced with the three cards to be transferred, stop the first man when he has counted to seven, and bend the sides of the cards downward, as they lie in the left hand. Then let him resume the count, with three more cards. This will let the three cards rest separately on top of the heap, ready for the toss.

Be sure that the man who is to receive the handkerchief is on your extreme right. Thrust your elbow close to his face, so that he cannot see the transfer. The other spectators will not see it, as your arm and body are turned away.

Be sure that the cards are clearly counted before and after the trick, so that the effectiveness of the mystery will not be lost.

Variation: In this method, the man on the left uses red-backed cards; the man on the right uses blue-backed cards. Yet the trick takes place, and three red cards are found among the blue!

The right hand has a more difficult task in this form of the trick. The cards are rested on the fingers; and as you turn to the right, the right thumb must lift a few of the cards, making an opening into which the cards from the left hand slide. The right hand instantly squares its cards, showing a blue back still on top. The trick then proceeds in the usual manner. The three red cards are found among the blue.

By way of increasing the effectiveness, you may lay the right hand cards face up in the handkerchief, after displaying the blue back on top. When the handkerchief is opened, tell the man on your right to shuffle them face up, to see if they feel like thirteen. This mixes the reds among the blues, and when he finally turns them over and counts them on your hand, the red cards make their appearance at different places.

The actions of the hands may be reversed, if desired, the right hand making the throw instead of the left.

12. BLACKSTONE'S KING AND QUEEN

Three cards, queen, king and deuce are shown, and this little story is unfolded:

"Many years ago there lived a king and queen on the Isle of Bong. She was very fond of him, but one day she became rather peeved, and gave him the deuce (1) for no other reason than that he came home with his hair dyed red (2) and her thoughts were of another queen who had told him to do this. So the king in turn became peeved, and leaving her with the deuce, went away —never to return."

At this point, the king becomes a blank card.

There are three cards used in the trick; a deuce, a blank, and a queen. But the queen is a faked card; for on the right half of it, you paste the face of a king.

When the three cards are exhibited, the blank card is placed in back of the deuce, and the two are placed over the side of the faked card, so that the cards appear to be fanned—queen, king and deuce. (1) Point to the deuce.

When the backs of the cards are shown, the thumb of the hand slides the deuce aside, showing the back of the blank card, which is taken to be the back of the king. It should be red-backed, and the others should preferably be another color.

This draws attention from the spreading action, and naturally explains why the backs are shown (2).

Draw out the blank and lay it face down on the table. Slide the deuce under the face of the faked card so that it hides the portion of the king pasted thereon. Show the two cards back and front and pocket them. The "king" on the table proves to be a blank.

13. THE TURNING CARD

A very clever feat with prepared cards is performed with three cards—two spots and a face card.

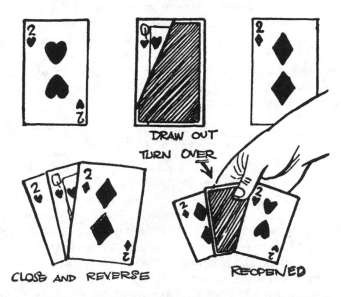

DRAW OUT
TURN OVER

CLOSE AND REVERSE   REOPENED

The picture card is shown between the other two. Then the fan is closed, and the cards are turned over. When they are spread again, the picture card is face up, while the others are back up! Yet all three cards are shown separately back and front.

Preparation: Cut a good-sized corner from a duplicate picture card, and paste it to the upper left corner of the back of the genuine card.

This enables you to show three cards in a fan—the face card between the others—but with the face card actually back up. The backs of the cards are not shown.

The fan is closed. The cards are turned over, and also turned around, so that the fan is formed from the other end. The genuine face of the picture card shows between the backs of other cards. Turning the fan over, the back of the picture card is seen between the faces of the spot cards—the fake corner still being hidden in the fan, under one of the spot cards.

Now comes the clever maneuver. Seize the end of the picture card, and draw the card quickly from the fan, at the same instant turning it face upward. Slap it down on the table. This action makes it appear that you have shown the card back and front—apart from the other two cards, whereas you have not shown the back completely.

Then turn the spot cards over, one at a time, and drop them faces down on the table. You have shown three separate and distinct cards—back and front.

14. BLACKSTONE'S MASTERPIECE PACK

Some years ago, this pack of cards was planned, and it has still retained its value of general utility to the average magician.

The pack utilizes two "key" cards—one shorter than the other cards in the pack; the other narrower. These can be prepared with a pair of scissors; but it is best to trim them with a photographic cutter, and have the corners carefully rounded afterward. About 1/32 of an inch is cut off.

This pack will stand inspection; it can be used in ordinary card games; yet when tricks are in order, it will be very easy to perform them.

The pack may be shuffled and a card selected. When the pack is laid on the table, the magician takes it by the sides and lifts off some of the cards. His fingers finding the break at the narrow card naturally lift all cards above that point, and the chosen card goes on the narrow one.

The pack may be cut frequently; but the performer has merely to cut at the narrow card again, and he will show the chosen card on the bottom of the portion he has lifted.

A second card may also be controlled with the aid of the short card; in this instance the performer cuts at the end instead of the sides.

An effective trick is to have a card taken from the pack. Then riffle the ends of the cards, inviting return of the selected card. As the riffle reaches the short card, it will suddenly stop, and the selected card will go back on top of the short one. After the pack has been cut several times, remove any card, and push it face upward into the pack. Do this at the end, and make sure that it goes in just above the short card. Thus when you run through the pack, the chosen card will be face to face with the upturned card.

To "force" the short card, get it to the middle of the pack. Riffle the ends of the pack very rapidly, inviting a person to thrust his finger in the cards as they fall. Start the riffle as his finger approaches. He will have difficulty inserting his finger until the short card brings the riffle to a sudden stop. Advance the pack at that instant and catch his finger.

This movement is bold but effective, and he will be sure his choice was free. Tell him to look at the card below his finger. Naturally he sees the short card. He may then shuffle the pack to his heart's content. As soon as you cut at the end of the pack, you will bring the chosen (and "forced") card to the top.

Worked in combination, the short and narrow cards produce some amazing results. Here is the feature trick with this pack.

Have the short card on top; the narrow card on the bottom. Let a spectator count off any number of cards—say sixteen—face down on the table, while your back is turned. This action reverses the cards counted; so when he replaces them, the short card will be the sixteenth from the top.

The pack may then be cut several times. When you take the pack, find the narrow card and cut at that point, so that it is on the bottom again. Then riffle the ends to find the short card. Lift off the short card and all above it. Count the cards and you will have sixteen—the exact number he counted! They are actually the spectator's cards.

15. CORNER BENDING

One of the neatest—and easiest—principles of modern card conjuring is that of the "bent corner."

When a card is chosen from an ordinary pack, the performer secretly bends the inner corner with the fingers of his right hand.

This may be done while a spectator is pointing to the card he desires to select; or it may be performed after the card has been returned to the spread out pack. The fingers of the right hand, under the pack, accomplish the action with very little difficulty.

No matter how much the pack is shuffled, the chosen card can always be discovered by looking at the corners; and it can be brought to top or bottom by cutting the pack there.

The cleverest trick dependent on this principle is to insert a card face up under the bent corner, and to lift the cards there, showing the one selected. This may be varied by showing two cards face up, and thrusting one in below the bent corner; and the other above. When the cards are withdrawn, the chosen card comes between them.

Or it may be done thus: Show a card and ask: "Is that your card?" When "No" is answered, say: "Remember this card." Put it in the pack face down, under the bent corner. Do the same with another card, and put it over the bent corner.

Then turn the pack face up, and spread the cards, asking everyone to watch for the two cards just shown. When they are observed, the chosen card will be seen between them.

16. THE MYSTIC REVERSO

This trick is quite new in principle, and has never been described in print. It requires practice, but can be easily acquired.

In effect, a card is chosen from a fan and is replaced in the pack. A card is withdrawn, but it is not the chosen one; so the pack is cut, and the chosen card is found face up among the others.

First obtain a pack with white margins on the backs. This is essential. Now reverse one of the spot cards and insert it about sixteen from the top.

Fan the pack from right to left—opposite to the usual direction. The cards are fanned very slightly at the top of the pack—just enough so that you can detect the reversed card by its slightly wider margin.

After a card is chosen from below, where the cards are spread more widely, take the card from the chooser and push it face down in the pack—directly above the turned-up card.

Square the pack, and state that you will find the chosen card. Riffle the cards slightly until you see the reversed card. Cut the pack one card below it.

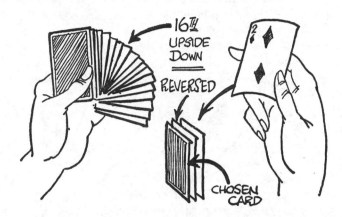

Thus on the bottom of the pack you will have first an indifferent card (say the two of clubs); next the turned-up card; and then the chosen card.

Hold the bottom of the pack toward yourself, and carefully remove the three bottom cards as one. Do this by sliding them off slightly, and squaring them. Show this card—which appears to be the deuce of clubs—back and front, keeping the hand in motion as you do so, so that no one will detect the unusual thickness of the card.

Lay this "card" face up on top of the pack, and remark that it should be the chosen card. The reply is made that it is not.

Remove the deuce of clubs alone, and push it into the center of the pack, face down. This leaves the card that was formerly the turned-up card face down on top of the pack. The second card will be the chosen one—face up. Allow the pack to be cut, and when you spread the cards, you will reveal the chosen card—face up.

17. CARD THROUGH HANDKERCHIEF—AND CASE

Very few magicians know this excellent trick—an improvement upon the old "Card Through Handkerchief." In this version, a chosen card is shuffled into the pack; the pack is put in the case; the case is wrapped in a handkerchief, and the card comes through both case and handkerchief.

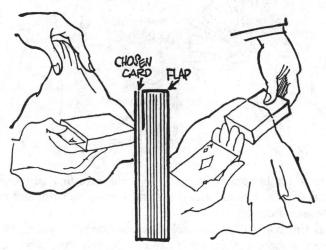

Illustrating the removal of the chosen card from the case; also how the flap is set under the chosen card.

The procedure is as follows: First bring the chosen card to the top of the pack, and put the pack in the case, which should be of the usual variety—with a flap—not a fancy box.

Put the pack in the case so that the top card is away from the flap. Then close the flap, and in so doing, insert it between the top card and the rest of the pack—a natural easy action. Then you show the case on all sides, keeping your thumb over the semicircular cut that is in front of the flap, and which might reveal a portion of the back of the chosen card.

Take the case in the right hand, holding the back of the case toward the spectators. The case is at the finger tips, and the second finger touches the projecting back of the chosen card.

Throw the handkerchief over the case, and as you do so, draw the chosen card out an inch, so that it may be firmly clipped between the side of the thumb and the hand.

With the left hand, reach beneath the cloth and bring out the case, leaving the chosen card in the right hand. Put the case on the handkerchief, so that it lays directly over the card hidden beneath.

Fold up the lower portion of the handkerchief, over the case. Then grip the case and the card beneath, with the thumb and second finger of the left hand. This lets the right hand fold one side of the handkerchief underneath the chosen card; then the pack lays on the right hand. The left hand takes the other side of the cloth, including the portion just folded under by the right, and folds it back the other way.

This simple procedure of winding the handkerchief about the pack forms a pocket which conceals the chosen card and the handkerchief may be shown from both sides, while the loose corners are held at the top.

When the handkerchief is shaken, the chosen card will gradually come loose and will make its appearance through the cloth, dropping to the floor. Then case—handkerchief—cards—everything may be thoroughly examined by the audience.

18. THE HUNG CARD

The principle of this trick is so simple, that it can be performed with nothing but a piece of string. But in its elaborate form, the string is attached to a miniature gallows.

A card is selected and returned to the pack. The pack is inserted in a loop in the end of the string. One card in the pack—namely, the chosen card—is the culprit; and it must be executed.

With a simple piece of string, the pack is shaken loose and all the cards fall except the chosen one, which hangs there. With the gallows, a trap is pulled and all the pack falls through—except the chosen card.

In the improved gallows, the release of the trap raises the top portion of the gallows, so that the card comes upward as the pack falls, making the appearance more effective.

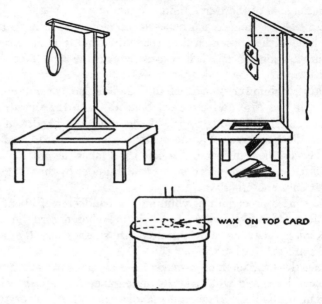

WAX ON TOP CARD

Yet the simplicity of method is used in each instance. The loop is of fairly heavy string; and a dab of wax (or lead plaster) is attached to it. The chosen card is brought to the top of the pack. The pack is slipped into the loop, and under pretense of tightening the loop, the portion of the string that bears the wax is pressed firmly against the back of the chosen card.

The pack hangs in the string, but the loop is not tight. A slight shake will release the pack, leaving the chosen card hanging in the loop. With the gallows arrangement, the loop is quite loose so that the pack will surely drop when the trap is released.

19.   DIVINATION CARD TRICKS

There are three clever ways of divining a chosen card apparently hidden from view. These may be worked separately or in combination. I shall describe each one in brief.

(A) X-Ray Pack

Half of the cards of a pack are prepared by having the index corners punched out. This is concealed with the thumb. Any card is inserted among the fake cards, which are held face down. When the performer turns the faces of the cards toward himself, he lifts his thumb and sees the index corner of the chosen card.

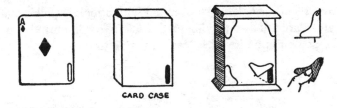

CARD CASE

(B) X-Ray Case

This is merely a card case with the proper corner cut out, and hidden by the thumb. A card is dropped into the case. By turning the faked side toward him and lifting his thumb the performer will see the chosen card.

(C) X-Ray Box

This is an excellent piece of apparatus—a wooden box with a loose lid, large enough to hold a playing card. The corners are ornamental raised pieces. All appear tight, so the box may pass examination. But when he turns the box toward himself, the performer pushes upward on the lower right corner piece. This raises a pin from a small hole in the bottom of the box, and the corner pivots inward, giving a glimpse of the concealed card—a glimpse of the tell-tale index corner.

The ornamental piece is swung back and pressed down into place. Then the performer names the chosen card.

Two of these methods may be worked together—or all three may be combined to make a more remarkable illusion.

20. THE LATEST CARD BOX

The card box is an apparatus of utility for causing the appearance, disappearance, or change of a card. The old wooden box has a flap in the top that falls into the bottom, and it has become generally known. The nickeled card box is a piece of apparatus that can be examined; but its size and weight are suspicious. The "Latest Card Box" is very thin.

It consists of a single piece of metal with a molding all around it—slightly larger than a playing card. It has two thin hinged doors, which open on opposite sides, each opening to the right.

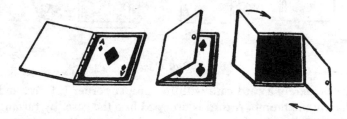

Thus there are two compartments, one on either side of the box. One of the doors fits loosely, and has a knob on it; the other is tight fitting, and cannot be opened except by striking the box forcibly against the hand. This door has no knob.

We will presume that the magician intends to transform a card with the aid of this box. He puts a red card in the side of the box that opens easily. Then he opens the other side, and lets the box lay in this condition.

He carries the opened box to a spectator and lets him place a black card in the box. He closes the door quickly, and transfers the box to his other hand. This enables him to exert sufficient pressure to lock the black card firmly in one side of the box.

When the spectator receives the box, and is told to open it, he naturally employs the door with the knob—the only door that he can see. There he finds the red card, and no trace of the black one. The original door has become the solid back of the box, and no one suspects its presence.

"El Barto," the well-known magician, utilizes the "Card Box" in combination with the "Card Through Handkerchief." He has a duplicate card in the pack—and "forces" one of these. This is the card that he shakes through the handkerchief. He places the card in a card box, from which it disappears. When the handkerchief is unwrapped, the card is discovered back in the pack.

The judicious combination of existing tricks is an excellent practice that leads to originality and effectiveness.

21. THE IMPROVED FALSE COUNT

This is a very effective form of the "False Count," executed slowly and deliberately.

The cards are held upright in the left hand, the faces of the cards toward the performer. The left thumb, touching the face of the card nearest the performer, pushes it to the right, where it is removed by the right hand.

This is repeated with the second card; the third card; and so on, but the cards retain their same relative position; that is, the cards in the right hand are placed upon each succeeding card as it is drawn off.

Now in the course of slowly removing one of the cards from the left hand, the right hand pushes the nearest card of its group back to the left, where it is gripped by the left thumb. This takes place while the hands are momentarily together; the slide back of the card is completely masked by the other cards, which are unevenly spread in the hands.

This secretly adds one card to the left hand group; and by repeating the maneuver more cards may be added, one by one, to the group in the left hand.

Thus with seven cards in his left hand, the magician may count ten, thus: one, two, three (slide back), four, five (slide back), six, seven (slide back), eight, nine, ten.

Nine, or eight may also be counted by merely sliding back one or two cards less.

The "False Count." Note how the first card is transferred from right to left during the count. Spectators see the backs of the cards.

While this sleight may be done very slowly, it should be practiced to do at a moderately rapid speed, in which case it will be quite indetectible.

22. ACES UP

Simple, yet convincing, this is a real baffler. The magician shuffles a pack and hands it to a spectator, telling him to cut it into four nearly equal heaps, arranging them so they form the corners of a square.

He is then to pick up the first heap and deal three cards on the corner where it was. From that same heap he must next deal single cards on the other heaps, three in all, going around the square. He then drops the heap on the three cards he first dealt.

This same routine is followed with the second heap, then the third, and finally the fourth, all cards being dealt face down. Three to a corner—one to each heap—then drop the packet where it was. At the finish, the spectator is told to turn up the top card of each heap. To his amazement, he finds that they are the four aces!

Start with the aces on top of the pack and the trick will work automatically. Naturally, they should be placed there beforehand, without the spectator's knowledge. The pack may be given a riffle shuffle, always letting the top cards fall slower than the rest, so they stay where they belong.

The "first" heap is the bottom one; the "fourth" is the original top heap. Make sure the spectator deals from them in that order as he goes around the square, heap by heap.

23. FLIGHTY

A spectator selects a card and replaces it in the pack, which is promptly shuffled by the magician. All the while, the person is told to concentrate upon his card, which he alone knows.

To reveal the chosen card in a novel manner, the magician grips the pack in his left hand and gives the outer end a forceful riffle, with the fingers of his right. Out from the pack shoots a tiny card—about a quarter the size of a regular playing card. The spectator names his card, say "Six of Hearts" and the miniature card matches it!

Simple sleights are utilized in this real "eye-popper," as such effects are termed. The original card—the big six of hearts—is forced, as earlier described in this chapter. While the card is being noted, the performer turns away and obtains the tiny duplicate from his pocket, holding the miniature card in the bend of his left fingers, where it is hidden beneath the pack.

The chosen card is replaced and by means of the overhand shuffle, the magician shuffles the duplicate miniature into the pack itself. By gripping the pack tightly at the inner end and riffling the outer ends of the cards very sharply, the little six spot will be scaled from the pack, to the surprise of the spectators.

If it misses on the first riffle, a few more snaps will spring the card into sight.

24. PUSH

A highly intriguing card discovery, a real Blackstone favorite. Suppose the queen of hearts has been selected. The magician holds the pack with a card projecting from one end, such as the ace of spades, and asks: "Is that your card?"

The chooser says, "No," so the magician remarks: "We'll push it through the pack and see what happens." Pushed through, the card comes out the other end of the pack as an entirely different card, say the ten of clubs.

Though surprised, the spectator still insists it is not his card. So the magician gives it another push through the pack and this time it emerges as the chosen queen of hearts, which is handed to the baffled chooser.

Five cards are used for this series of "changes," with the chosen card—which the magician first locates by any suitable method— as the middle card of the group. However, in fixing the cards, the magician pushes the first, third, and fifth cards well forward, letting the second and fourth project backward from the group.

The group is then placed in the center of the pack, so that the retarded cards (second and fourth) are exactly flush with the pack itself. The projecting cards (first, third, and fifth) are then squared to appear as a single card. Gripping the pack rather firmly in one hand, the magician shows the facing card of the projecting group, say the ace of spades.

When the spectator says "No," the wizard pushes the whole group down into the pack. This causes the second and fourth cards to emerge together from the other end. Apparently, the ace of spades has changed into the ten of clubs (the fourth card).

Another push in the opposite direction and the center card

emerges alone. Not only is the change surprising, it proves to be the chosen queen of hearts, which can be handed for inspection as a single card.

25. WHIRLY

The ultimate in card discoveries. Several cards are laid in a circle, one being a selected card. The magician introduces a thin, flat strip of metal, which has a slight hump in the center, so it can be balanced at that spot. The strip is like a bodkin or flattish needle, except for the hump, which enables the magician to give it a spin, after it has been placed in the center of the card circle.

In fact, the spectator himself may be allowed to twirl the improvised spindle, but all the while he is to concentrate upon his chosen card. After revolving uncontrolled, the little pointer pauses, wavers back and forth, finally stopping entirely, indicating one of the cards in the circle.

That card, when turned up, proves to be the chosen card!

Naturally, the magician must know the chosen card. He either forces it or locates it after it has been selected and returned to the pack. But how can he make the pointer indicate the card? Simply enough. The pointer is magnetized, so it is actually a compass needle. Revolved on a smooth surface, it will always finish pointing north.

The magician must first learn which direction is north. In laying out the circle, he places the chosen card at the northerly position. Anyone may then spin the innocent little metal pointer and it will be sure to stop on the chosen card, much to the mystification of the onlookers.

While the trick is perfect in that form, requiring no appliances other than the unsuspected compass needle, it is possible to control the pointer, particularly when a repeat is desired. This can be done by having a fairly powerful magnet concealed inside the card case, which is laid just beyond the selected card. The magnet will control the needle and cause it to point that way, so the selected card can be anywhere in the circle instead of to the north.

Sometimes the needle can be similarly controlled by arranging the circle of cards on a table near a telephone that is equipped with an interior magnet. In this case, the chosen card should be placed in the direction of the telephone, as it will control the action of the magic pointer.